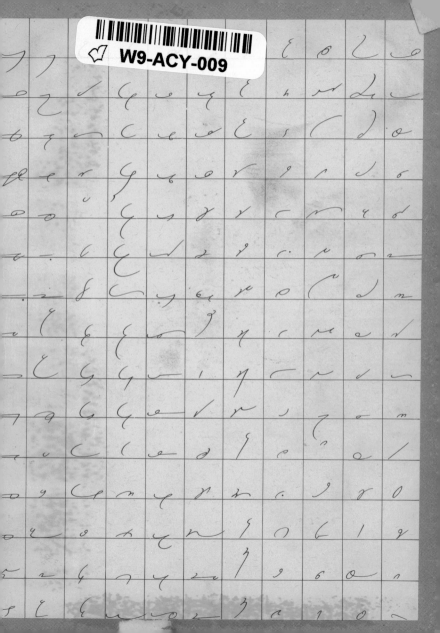

GREGG SHORTHAND

A LIGHT-LINE
PHONOGRAPHY
for the MILLION

By

JOHN ROBERT GREGG, S.C.D.

Anniversary Edition

THE GREGG PUBLISHING COMPANY

NEW YORK   CHICAGO   BOSTON   SAN FRANCISCO   TORONTO   LONDON   SYDNEY

PREFACE

Anyone who examines the Shorthand textbooks of the last three centuries will be impressed with the fact that they have reflected the uses to which shorthand was put at the time the books were written.

The pedagogy of shorthand has changed as radically as the content of the textbooks. Up to the time Gregg Shorthand was introduced, the conventional pedagogy was to teach the theory of a system as a whole before attempting to apply the theory in the actual writing of connected matter. While the system would undoubtedly have made its way into public favor by its own inherent strength, we believe that its success and progress throughout the world have been hastened enormously by the teachability of its textbooks.

In keeping with the progress in business and in education, the Gregg Manual was revised in 1893, 1901, and 1916, this latter edition being the one used at present. Each revision marked a step forward in simplifying and popularizing the study of shorthand. Each revision has placed increasing emphasis upon the desirability of teaching shorthand as a *skill subject* from the beginning and throughout the entire course. This method enables the teacher to direct the maximum of effort toward the training of the student in actual facility in writing and the minimum of effort to expositions of rules and principles.

When it became known that a revision of the Manual was in preparation, hundreds of protests were received from teachers. Many of them declared emphatically that the 1916 edition was entirely adequate. A great many said that they "love it" (this expression occurs again and again in their letters) and that they "know it by heart." The sentiments expressed are thoroughly appreciated, and all these good friends are assured that it will still be possible to obtain the 1916 edition as long as there is any demand for it.

In this new edition no changes have been made in the *basic principles of the system*. Long experience in the classroom, in the office, in general and court reporting, and the results of speed contests of the National Shorthand Reporters' Association have proved conclusively that changes in the basic principles of Gregg Shorthand are neither necessary nor desirable.

Much has been learned in the last few years concerning the basic content of the vocabulary in common use. The scientific data now available have made it possible to arrange the principles and practice content of the Manual so that the efforts of teacher and student may be more economically and profitably directed, and the development of a writing vocabulary rendered more rapid.

One of the first steps in planning the Anniversary Edition, therefore, was an exhaustive analysis of the words contained in the Horn* and the Harvard† studies of the comparative frequency of words. As one example of what this analysis showed, it was found that the learning of the twenty most common words in our language was spread through seven lessons in the 1916 Manual. In the Anniversary Edition these twenty words are presented in the first chapter. Moreover, the matter presented in this chapter gives the student a writing power that will enable him to write 42 per cent of the running words in non-technical English, as well as many hundreds of other words.

In this edition three devices have been used to hasten the building of a useful vocabulary and to assist the teacher in using the correct method of developing a skill subject:

---

*"Basic Writing Vocabulary," Ernest Horn, Ph.D., University of Iowa Monograph in Education.

†"Harvard Studies in Education," Volume IV.

1. The short words of high frequency are introduced in the first chapter in the order of their frequency, even though this means that in a few instances they are given in advance of the principles that govern their writing.

2. Some of the principles have been developed earlier than they were in the old text. Examples of this are: the letter *s* has been introduced in the second chapter and included with the other downward characters; some of the rules for expressing *r* have been introduced in the third chapter; the frequently recurring prefixes and suffixes have been introduced in the order of frequency.

3. Analogy, one of the most helpful of teaching devices, has been employed to a greater extent than it was in the 1916 Manual. Examples: the useful *ted-ded*, *men-mem* blends are presented in Chapter I, after the student has learned *t*, *d*, *n*, *m*, the letters of which the blends are composed; the *ses* blend is taught along with the *s* in Chapter II.

Other salient features of the Anniversary Edition may be described as follows:

1. In order that the student may be impressed at the outset with the importance of phrase writing and have a longer period in which to acquire the habit of joining words, many of the phrasing principles have been moved forward to Chapters I and II.

2. The rules have been simplified and stated more clearly, and minor changes have been made in a few outlines for the purpose of facilitating rapid and accurate transcription.

3. The principles are presented in twelve chapters, instead of the twenty lessons in the 1916 Manual. Each of these chapters has been subdivided into three short teaching units, with a page of graded dictation material written in shorthand at the end of each unit. This short-unit plan encourages immediate practical application of the theory and simplifies the assignment of work by the teacher.

4. The wordsigns (now known as Brief Forms) are distributed equally among the first six chapters, and are introduced in the order of their frequency.

5. The quantity of reading and dictation material has been more than doubled. The scientific distribution of the principles and the introduction of the common words early have so greatly increased writing power that business letters can be introduced as early as the second chapter.

6. The pedagogical value of the Manual is greatly enhanced by the use of larger type and a bolder style of shorthand than was employed in the 1916 edition.

It was the intention of the author to have the Anniversary Edition of the system published last year—the fortieth anniversary of the publication of the system—but, unfortunately, many things contributed to delay its appearance.

In sending forth this book he desires to express his warm appreciation of the many suggestions received from writers, from reporters, and from teachers who are using the system in all parts of the world. In particular, he wishes to record his deep sense of gratitude to Mr. Rupert P. SoRelle and to the executive, managerial, and editorial staffs of The Gregg Publishing Company for the many valuable services they have rendered in the preparation of this edition.

JOHN ROBERT GREGG.

ABOUT GREGG SHORTHAND

History. Gregg Shorthand was first published in 1888, in two little paper-covered pamphlets, under the title, "Light-Line Phonography." Five years later, a revised and greatly improved edition was published under the title, "Gregg Shorthand." It was not until 1897, however, that the author was able to publish the system in *book* form.

To the student or writer of shorthand, there are few more interesting or inspiring stories of success than the story of the career of Gregg Shorthand in the thirty-two years that have elapsed since its publication in book form; but a textbook is not a place for such a story.. Today, Gregg Shorthand is the standard system of America. It has been adopted exclusively in the public schools of 6,519 cities and towns—more than ninety-seven per cent of the public schools that teach shorthand. It has superseded the older systems, in the large majority of these cases, by formal action of the Boards of Education after careful investigation of the merit of the system. Its leadership in all other kinds of educational institutions is equally pronounced. This constitutes the highest educational indorsement a shorthand system has ever received.

Wins World Championship Six Times. The history of Gregg Shorthand is a record of public triumphs. In the 1921 World's Championship Contest of the National Shorthand Reporters' Association, Mr. Albert Schneider* won first place, defeated three former champions, and established two world s records. He transcribed the 215-words-a-minute literary dictation with a net speed of 211.2 words a minute; accuracy, 98.32%. On the 200-words-a-minute dictation his accuracy percentage was 98.80; on the 240-words-a-minute dictation, 98.17; on the 280-words-a-minute dictation, 96.84.

In transcribing five five-minute highest speed dictations—175, 200, 215, 240, and 280 words a minute—*in the time allotted for the three championship*

---

*Mr. Schneider is now a member of the official shorthand reporting staff of the Congress of the United States, winning the position in an examination in which thirty-five well-known reporters competed.

dictations, Mr. Schneider gave one of the most remarkable demonstrations of transcribing ability in the history of the shorthand contests.

Writers of Gregg Shorthand won first, second, and third places in the World's Championship Contest of the National Shorthand Reporters' Association in 1923. Mr. Charles L. Swem,* winner, established a world's record on the 200-words-a-minute dictation, making but two errors; accuracy, 99.79%. On the 240-words-a-minute dictation, his accuracy was 98.49%; on the 280 dictation, 99.36%. Second place was won by Mr. Albert Schneider, a Gregg writer, the 1921 champion. His average accuracy was 98.80%. Third place was won by another Gregg writer, Mr. Martin J. Dupraw, with an accuracy of 98.76%. *First place in accuracy in every dictation was won by a writer of Gregg Shorthand.*

In the 1924 World's Championship, Mr. Swem was again the victor. Mr. Swem's accuracy on the three dictations was 99.23%.

In the three consecutive years, 1925, 1926, and 1927, the World's Shorthand Championship was won by Mr. Martin J. Dupraw, the greatest shorthand writer the world has yet produced. By winning the championship in 1927, Mr. Dupraw won permanent possession of the World's Shorthand Championship Trophy, first offered in 1909 by the National Shorthand Reporters' Association.

Highest Shorthand Speed Records. The following are the world's highest shorthand speed records—all held by writers of Gregg Shorthand and made in the Championship Contests of the National Shorthand Reporters' Association:

> 282 Words a minute (testimony)
> Charles Lee Swem . . . . accuracy 99.29%

---

*Governor Woodrow Wilson selected Mr. Swem as his official reporter in his campaign for the Presidency. Mr. Swem was Personal Secretary and Official Reporter to President Wilson for eight years. Mr. Swem began the study of Gregg Shorthand in a night school in September, 1908, when working as an office boy. He was twenty years of age when he received the appointment at the White House. In the 1924 examination for the position of Supreme Court stenographer in the state of New York, Mr. Swem won first place in a field of 150 candidates. Mr. Swem did not accept an appointment at the time, and took the examination in 1928, again winning first place. He is at present an official shorthand reporter in the Supreme Court of New York.

260 Words a minute (jury charge)
Martin J. Dupraw............accuracy 99.69%
220 Words a minute (literary matter)
Martin J. Dupraw............accuracy 99.81%
(Held jointly with two others)
215 Words a minute (literary matter)
Albert Schneider.............accuracy 98.32%
200 Words a minute (literary matter)
Charles Lee Swem............accuracy 99.0%
(Tied with one other)
Average accuracy 99.29%

Gregg Shorthand is the only system that has produced three different writers to win the World Championship in the contests of the National Shorthand Reporters' Association. The contests were discontinued in 1927, and Mr. Dupraw was given permanent possession of the World's Championship Trophy.

Wins New York State Shorthand Championship. In the contest of the New York State Shorthand Reporters' Association, 1924, Mr. Martin J. Dupraw won first place with an accuracy record of 99.5%; Mr. Nathan Behrin, Supreme Court reporter, New York City, second; and Mr. Harvey Forbes, Supreme Court reporter, Buffalo, New York, third. By winning the New York State Shorthand Championship again in 1925, and also in 1926, Mr. Dupraw gained permanent possession of the Bottome Cup, the State championship trophy.

Awarded Medal of Honor at Panama-Pacific Exposition. At the Panama-Pacific International Exposition, in 1915, Gregg Shorthand was awarded the Medal of Honor, the highest award ever granted a system of shorthand by any exposition, and the only award ever granted that was based on the results accomplished by students in a model school conducted under the observation of the International Jury of Awards. Gregg Shorthand also received the highest award, the Medal of Honor, at the Sesqui-Centennial Exposition at Philadelphia, in 1926. The thirteenth International Shorthand Congress, held in Bruxelles, Belgium, in 1927, awarded a *Grand Prix* to The Gregg Publishing Company, and elected the author of Gregg Shorthand as Vice President of the Congress representing the United States.

Principles of the System.   Needless to say, Gregg Shorthand is a radical departure from the old lines of shorthand construction, for it is only by a radical departure that such marked superiority in results can be accomplished.

The following is a synopsis of the leading features of the system:

1. *No compulsory thickening*—may be written either light or heavy.

2. *Written on the slope of longhand*, thus securing a uniform manual movement.

3. *Position-writing abolished*—may be written on unruled paper, and in one straight line.

4. *Vowels and consonants are joined*, and follow each other in their natural order.

5. *Angles are rare*—curves predominate.

As in ordinary writing

This brief synopsis will suffice to show that the aim of the author has been to adhere to those natural principles that govern ordinary writing. By a practical combination of these elements as a foundation, the system secures to the writer, *with very little practice*, that perfect command of the characters that is productive of the best results, and is obtained only by years of persistent, painstaking practice with the older systems.

TO SUM UP

Easy to Learn.   Gregg Shorthand may be learned in from one-third to one-half the time required by the old systems.   The records made by its writers prove this beyond all question.

Easy to Read.   Gregg Shorthand is the most legible shorthand in existence.   In the public shorthand speed contests, writers of the system have established the *highest official world's records for accuracy* of transcripts on difficult matter.   These records were made in competition with experienced reporters who used the older systems, and in contests conducted by reporters and teachers who wrote such systems.   Manifestly, the insertion of the vowels, the absence of shading, the elimination of position-writing, and the elimination of the minute distinctions of form, all contribute to legibility.

Easy to Write.   The easy, natural appearance of the writing in Gregg Shorthand appeals to every impartial investigator.   The absence of distinctions between light and heavy characters, the continuous run of the writing along one line, as in longhand, instead of constant changes of posi-

Gregg Shorthand received the highest award at the
Panama-Pacific International Exposition, and at
the Sesqui-Centennial International Exposition.

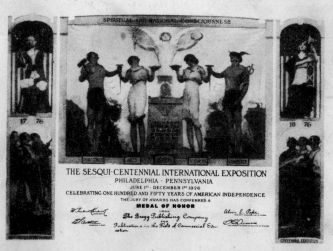

THE ALPHABET OF GREGG SHORTHAND

CONSONANTS

Written forward:

K G R L N M T D TH

⌐ ⌐ ⌐ ⌐ — — ╱ ╱ ⌐ or ╲

Written downward:

P B F V CH J S SH

(( )) ╱ ╱ ⌐ or ╱ ╱

H NG NK

• ⌐ ⌐

VOWELS

ă	○	ĭ	◦	ŏ	◡	ŭ	◠
ä	◯	ĕ	◦	aw	◡	ŏŏ	◠
ā	◯	ē	◦	ō	◡	ōō	◠

DIPHTHONGS

	Composed of			Composed of	
ū	ē-ōō as in *unit*	◌	oi	aw-ē as in *oil*	◌
ow	ä-ōō as in *owl*	◌	ī	ä-ē as in *isle*	○

BLENDED CONSONANTS

The consonants are so arranged that two strokes joining with an obtuse or blunt angle may assume the form of a large curve, thus:

ten, den	⌐	ent, end	╱	def-v, tive	◯
tem, dem	⌐	emt, emd	╱	jent-d, pent-d	◡

CHAPTER I

UNIT 1

1. Shorthand is written by *sound*; thus *aim* is written *am* (long sound of *a*), *cat* is written *kat*, *knee* is written *ne*.

CONSONANTS

2. The consonants are arranged in pairs, according to their affinity of sound, and are distinguished by a difference in length.

The characters for the consonants in this lesson are derived from an elliptical figure, thus:

Letters	Signs	Words	Letters	Signs	Words
K		can	T		it, at
G		go, good	D		would
R		are, our, hour	H		a, an
L		will, well	Th		the, there, their
N		in, not	O		I
M		am, more			he

3. All these consonants are written *forward* from left to right; *th* and *t* and *d* are struck *upwards* from the line of writing. The g given in this lesson is called *gay*, being the hard sound as in *game*, *get*, and not the soft sound heard in *gem*, *magic*. The aspirate *h* is indicated by a dot placed over the vowel. Many frequently recurring words are represented by simple alphabetic char-

I

acters. Some of these signs represent two and even three words; for example, the sign for *r* represents *are, our, hour*. A dot on the line of writing represents the articles *a, an*. A dot at the end of a word expresses *ing*. The pronoun *I* is expressed by a large circle; *he*, by a small circle.

The student should practice all these characters until he can write them without the slightest hesitation. The size of the characters given in this manual will be a safe standard to adopt.

4. Phrasing. The joining of simple words is a great help to accuracy and speed in writing shorthand, and its acquirement should not be deferred until the habit of writing common words separately has been formed.

I will ⌒⌒   he can ⌒   it will ⌒   in the ⌒

5. Punctuation, etc. In shorthand the following marks are used:

period	paragraph	interrogation	dash	hyphen	parenthesis
`	>	×	=	-	( )

Capitals and proper names are indicated by two short dashes beneath the word.

6. SENTENCE DRILL

VOWELS

7. In shorthand there are twelve distinct vowel sounds, which are arranged in four groups, and three closely related sounds are placed in each group. In this lesson we have the first two groups, which for convenience are named the A group and the E group.

Memory aid: a = ○ e = ·

THE A GROUP

ă	ä	ā
○	○	○
as in	*as in*	*as in*
mat	calm	came
mă t	kä m	kā m

THE E GROUP

ĭ	ĕ	ē
°	°	°
as in	*as in*	*as in*
kit	get	need
kĭ t	gĕ t	nē d

NOTE: The first sound in the E group of vowels is the short *i*, heard in *din*, and should not be confused with long *i*, heard in *dine*, which will be given later.

8. Marking Vowels. The vowels are grouped according to similarity in sound. The large circle expresses three sounds of *a*. The short sound is unmarked, the medium sound is marked with a dot, and the long sound with a short dash, as shown on page 3. This system of marking is used in all vowel groups uniformly.

The dot and dash are occasionally needed to indicate the exact sounds in unfamiliar or isolated words, but otherwise they are seldom used.

PICTURING WRITING MOTION

9. Frequently we shall have to refer to writing motion. The curved characters in this lesson are taken from horizontal ovals, one written with *right* motion, the other with *left*.

Right motion: *Left motion:*

10. Characters taken from the left-motion oval are called *left-motion*, because the rotation is *from left to right*; characters taken from the right-motion oval are called *right-motion* for a like reason; thus:

K-G *are*
right-motion strokes   R-L *are*
left-motion strokes

The terms "left motion" and "right motion" refer to the *rotation* in movement, and not to the *direction*.

HOW CIRCLES ARE JOINED

The following movement drills are intended to develop skill in the joining of circles.

11. Circles Joined to Single Strokes.   At the beginning or end of a single curve, the circle is placed *inside* the curve:

eke		ear		array	
egg		ill		airy	
ache		air		alley	
key		ail		hack	
gay		ray		hag	

12. At the beginning or end of a single straight stroke, the circle is written with *right* motion:

aim		tea		ham	
ate		day		heat	
add		may		head	
eat		me		heed	
hid		eddy		hate	

13. READING AND DICTATION PRACTICE

(shorthand outlines)

UNIT 2

14. Circles Between Strokes. Where an angle, or a point, is formed at the junction of consonants, the circle goes outside the angle:

kick		make		rain	
cake		met		rim	
get		maid		tale	
gate		team		rainy	
calm		rear		dream	

15. Where straight strokes and curves join without an angle, or where two similar-motion curves join without an angle, the circle is placed inside the curve:

writ		raid		dig	
rid		ticket		tag	
red		tack		taken	
read		take		rattle	
rate		deck		riddle	

16. Some vowels are so obscure or neutral that they are omitted when they do not contribute to speed or legibility. For example, the *e* in the words

taken and *maker* is absolutely useless, and is omitted. Any vowel which does not contribute to the legibility of an outline may be omitted if its omission gives a more facile outline.

17. Between straight strokes in the same direction the circle is written with *right* motion:

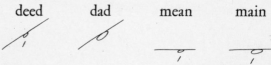

deed	dad	mean	main

18. Between opposite curves the circle is turned back on the first curve:

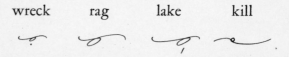

wreck	rag	lake	kill

CONSONANT COMBINATIONS

19. Kr and Gl Combinations. *K* and *r*, and *g* and *l*, are equal curves and are made a little flatter than usual when joined, thus:

kr ⁓　　　gl ⁓

cream	eagle	glen
crane	glee	glare
creed	glean	acre
crate	gleam	maker

20. Gr and Kl Combinations. Where curves of unequal length join without an angle, as in the following, note how a distinction in length is positively shown.

The movement in writing *gr* is similar to that in writing *y* in longhand; *kl* to that in writing *h*, thus:

= gr   = kl

gray		green		eager	
grain		greet		clay	
greed		grim		clan	

21. Rk and Lk Combinations. Since *r* and *k* are of equal length, the curves are somewhat flatter, as with *kr* and *gl*. *Lk* is very infrequent.

| ark | dark | mark | milk |

22. The Signs for Th. The sign for *t* is curved to express *th*, thus: or

| tick | thick | hat | hath |

| rat | wrath | met | myth |

BRIEF FORMS FOR COMMON WORDS

23. A comparatively small number of frequently recurring words make up a large part of the English language. As an illustration, ten words—*the, of, and, to, a, in, that, it, is, I*—form one-fourth of the entire written and spoken language.

The forms for these frequent words are based on a very common method of abbreviation in longhand writing. For example, *amt.* is written for *amount*; *Rev.* for *Reverend*; *gym.* for *gymnasium*; *ans.* for *answer*; *math.* for *mathematics*, and so on. By taking advantage of this method of abbreviation, brief and easily remembered shorthand forms are obtained for the most common words in the language.

of		and, end		them	
(o)		*(nd)*		*(thm)*	
that		to, too, two		is, his	
(tha)		*(too)*		*(s)*	
was		be, by, but		great	
(os)		*(b)*		*(gr)*	
they*		you, your		with	
(the)		*(oo)*		*(ith)*	
this		than, then		without	
(ths)		*(thn)*		*(itht)*	

*In some phrases *they* is written the same as *the*, as in *they will*.
NOTE: Refer to alphabet facing page 1 for explanation of characters.

24. BUSINESS ABBREVIATIONS

Mr., market   Yours truly,   Dear Sir:, desire

25. READING AND DICTATION PRACTICE

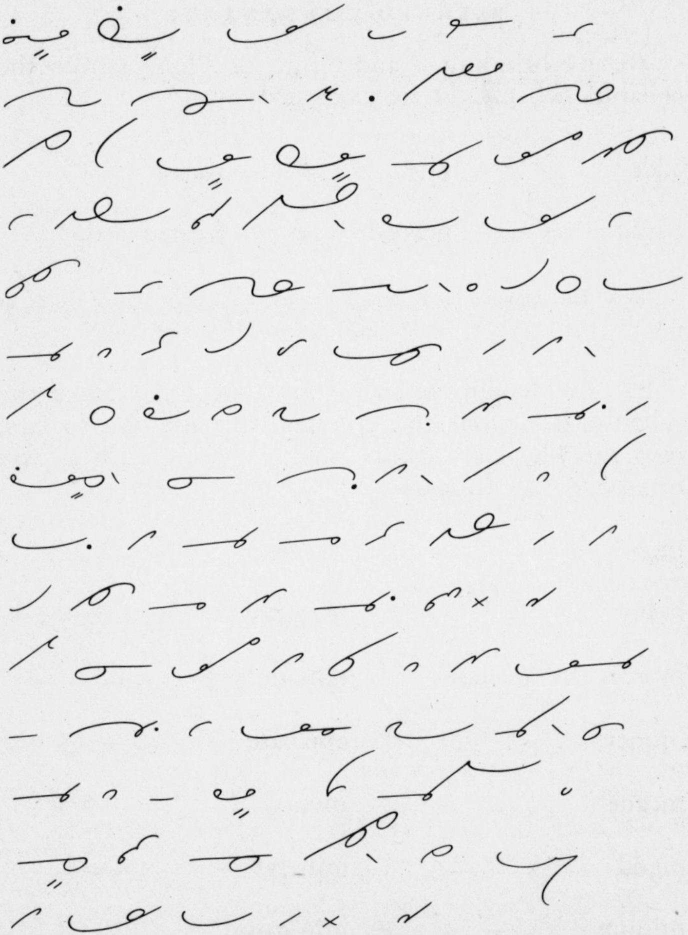

UNIT 3

BLENDED CONSONANTS

26. By blending *d* and *t* into one long stroke the syllables *ted*, *ded*, *det* are expressed:

added		rated		today	
hated		needed		treated	

NOTE: The combination *det* usually occurs at the beginning of words, as in *detect*, *detach*, while *ted* or *ded* usually occurs at the end of a word.

27. By blending *m* and *n* into one long stroke the syllables *men*, *mem* are expressed. In addition to *men*, *mem* this blend represents similar sounds, such as *min* in *minute*, *mun* in *money*:

men		mimic	
many		memory	
month		remain	
money		emanate	
meant		mental	
mend		mineral	
minute		minimum	

28. FREQUENT-WORD DRILL

eight	ā t		man	m ă n
had	h ă d		make	m ā k
him	h ĭ m		tin	t ĭ n
add	ă d		tan	t ă n
aid	ā d		cat	k ă t
tea	t ē		kid	k ĭ d
day	d ā		get	g ĕ t
me	m ē		take	t ā k
may	m ā		came	k ā m
net	n ĕ t		her	h ĕ r
need	n ē d		here	h ē r
met	m ĕ t		air	ā r
meet	m ē t		head	h ĕ d
made	m ā d		read	r ē d
mean	m ē n		ready	r ĕ d ĭ

led	l ĕ d		cream	k r ē m	
rate	r ā t		clean	k l ē n	
late	l ā t		milk	m ĭ l k	
laid	l ā d		lack	l ă k	
mill	m ĭ l		leg	l ĕ g	
tree	t r ē		attack	ă t ă k	
train	t r ā n		headache	h ĕ d ā k	

29. BRIEF FORMS FOR COMMON WORDS

did, date		when		into	
other		any		come	
all		could		like	
were		what		little	
where, aware		truth		those	
my		time		country	

Note: *W* is omitted in the word *were*, and *wh* in *where*, *when*, *what*; *other* is expressed by *ŭth*—see alphabet; *all*, by *aw* placed on its side; *time*, by the *tem* blend; *into*, by blending *in* and *to*. For convenience, the long *i* in *my* is expressed by a large circle.

GENERAL PHRASING PRINCIPLES

30. The following suggestions will be helpful to an understanding of the general principles of phrasing:

1. Short and common words only should be joined, as *of the*, *in the*, etc.

2. The words should make good sense if standing alone, as *it will be*.

3. Pronouns generally are joined to the words they precede, as *I can*, *you are*, *you can*, *I would*.

4. A qualifying word is usually joined to the word it qualifies, as *good man*.

5. The words *to*, *of*, *in*, *with*, and generally are joined to the word following, as *to the*, *of which*, *in that*, *with that*, *and will*.

6. Words that do not make an easily written, distinctive joining should not be phrased.

31. Phrase Drill. The simple phrases given in the drill below are of very high frequency and will serve as models for other phrases:

of the	and the	will be
to the	that the	of you
it is	by the	it was
I am	you can	he was
to you	at the	is the

32. READING AND DICTATION PRACTICE

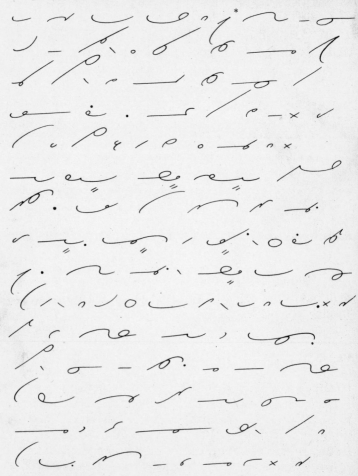

*Before a downstroke, *to* is expressed by *t*.

33. WRITING PRACTICE

1. You will need a keen memory when you go to the market today.

2. When you take the grain to the mill you can get your money.

3. Many of our men will go to the train in the rain to greet the team.

4. I am not any more eager to be in debt to you than you are.

5. I am ready to go the limit in getting you the money you need.

6. He had a great desire to read, but he had little time and his reading was limited.

7. I am not willing to go by train, but you can make me a minimum rate by air and rail.

8. The data you need will be ready by the middle of the month.

9. The mill was then making a good metal tag at the rate of eighty a minute.

10. In his dream he was being attacked in the dark by an enemy.

Dear Sir: I am eager to eliminate without any more delay the error made in the minimum grain rate to Erie. I can meet you at Erie any day you desire. My time is limited and I cannot be there more than a day. It would be well to get all the data in hand by the time you are ready to go. I will meet you any day you can be there. Yours truly,

CHAPTER II

UNIT 4

THE DOWNWARD CHARACTERS

34. The characters for the consonants in this chapter are derived from another elliptical figure:

Letters	P	B	F	V	CH	J	SH	S
Signs	(	(	)	)	/	/	,	، or ,

Words	put	be by but	for	have	which change		shall ship	is his

Left motion: P B S

Right motion: F V S

35. All these characters are written downward. *Ch* is named *chay*, and *sh* is named *ish*. The signs for *sh* and *s* are very small. As *s* is one of the most frequent sounds in the language, two signs are provided for it to facilitate joining in various combinations. The following memory aids will be useful:

CONSONANT COMBINATIONS

36. Many of the consonants follow each other consecutively; for example, *r* and *l* frequently follow *p*, *b*, as in *play*, *brave*.   As skill in writing such combinations is essential to speed and accuracy, the following movement drills should be practiced until fluency is secured.

37. Pr and Pl. In writing *pr* and *pl*, start to the left:

pr ⌒   pl ⌒

pray	⌒	play	⌒	pledge	⌒
prayer	⌒	plate	⌒	wrapper	⌒
prim	⌒	plea	⌒	pepper	⌒
preach	⌒	plead	⌒	apple	⌒

38. Br and Bl. In writing *br* and *bl*, start down, thus:

br ⌒   bl ⌒

brain	⌒	breach	⌒	blame	⌒
braid	⌒	bridge	⌒	bled	⌒
braided	⌒	brief	⌒	blade	⌒
brim	⌒	brave	⌒	blare	⌒

39. Fr and Fl. In writing the combinations *fr* and *fl*, the angle is rounded to give fluency. The motion is just the same as in writing a part of the longhand *y*:

		fr =		fl =	
fray		fresh		flame	
frail		flee		flap	
fret		fleet		flash	

40. FREQUENT-WORD DRILL

if		frame		page	
half		flat		able	
age		play		break	
each		plan		cash	
she		paper		range	
fear		reach		happy	
feel		back		black	
felt		check		trip	
free		live		happen	

fair	*⟋*	bear	*⟋*	help	*⟋*
affair	*⟋*	bread	*⟋*	labor	*⟋*
fail	*⟋*	shape	*⟋*	pretty	*⟋*
chief	*⟋*	leave	*⟋*	even	*⟋*

41. BRIEF FORMS FOR COMMON WORDS

one, won	*⟋*	from, form	*⟋*	never	*⟋*
after	*⟋*	been, bound	*⟋*	should	*⟋*
people	*⟋*	very	*⟋*	over*	....
about	*⟋*	before	*⟋*	ever	*⟋*
most	*⟋*	much	*⟋*	every	*⟋*

*The sign for the prefix *over* written above a following character is used to express the word *over*.

42. As a prefix, *after* is expressed by *af*. In compounds, *every* is expressed by *ev*.

43. The word *been* following *have*, *has*, *had* is phrased and is expressed by *b*:

have been   has been   had been

44. BUSINESS ABBREVIATIONS

Dear Madam: Very truly yours,   Yours very truly,

45. READING AND DICTATION PRACTICE

UNIT 5

THE SIGNS FOR S

46. The signs for *s*, written downward, are taken from a small elliptical figure, thus: ∮

Memory aid: ∮ ⸴

The right-motion *s* is called "right *s*"   ⸴
The left-motion *s* is called "left *s*"   ⸜

47. In practical writing the sound of *z* is expressed by the sign for *s*, since no confusion arises from using the same character for both sounds in connected writing. We already are accustomed to writing and reading *s* for *z* in English, as in *rays, praise.*

It is *seldom* necessary to make a distinction between *s* and *z*, but when it is, a short dash is struck at a right angle to the sign for *s* to show that it has the sound of *z*, thus:

race ⸝   raise ⸝   gas ⟋   gaze ⟋

48. The base of the first consonant of a word rests on the line of writing, but when *s* precedes another consonant, the base of the consonant following the *s* is placed on the line.

49. Initial and Final S. 1. Before and after *p, b, r*, and *l*, and after *t, d, n, m*, and *o*, the left *s* is used:

sips	∮	phrase	⸝	daze	⸝
sables	⸜	slim	⸝	knees	⸝
series	⸜⸝	tease	⸝	mass	⟋

2. In all other cases the right *s* is used:

saves		seeds		sashes	
seeks		snap		sketches	
staff		smash		sages	

A circle placed outside the angle in any of these joinings does not change the motion.

50. FREQUENT-WORD DRILL

sell		spell		salary	
sale		spread		self	
piece		spare		trace	
pass		space		dress	
base		less		class	
busy		slip		crazy	
press		sleep		see	
praise		asleep		say	
place		sales		as	

has		same		steel	
these		sense		steam	
easy		seems		stage	
season		sit		stiff	
affairs		seat		stay	
safe		said		stick	
save		sad		set	
case		niece		sat	
kiss		miss		settle	
guess		days		silk	
gas		dance		needs	
sick		since		ladies	
sake		hence		chance	
scheme		minutes		ages	
seen		step		sketch	
seem		steps		study	

51. S Between Strokes. When a circle vowel immediately precedes *s* between strokes, treat the *s* as belonging to the preceding consonant; if the circle follows the *s*, the *s* should be treated as if it belonged to the following consonant; when *s* occurs between strokes and is not joined to a circle, write the *s* with the syllable to which it belongs:

cast		mask		least	
guest		grasp		risk	
taste		accede		pressed	
task		chest		raised	
desk		vast		ransack	
mist		visit		mason	

52. The Ses Sign. The *ses* sound as heard in *faces* is expressed by joining the two *s* signs as a blend:

senses		ceases		basis	
cases		thesis		census	
masses		traces		analysis	

NOTE: In rapid writing, the first *s* in *ses* may become obscure, and yet the second *s*, being written contrary to the rule for writing a single *s*, clearly indicates the plural form. Compare the following:

face   faces   lease   leases

53. BRIEF FORMS FOR COMMON WORDS

under*	....	cause, because		work		
must		thorough-ly, three		part		
some		think, thing		matter		
such		system, says		again		
first		public, publish		against		
business		far, favor		always		

*The sign for the prefix *under* written above a following character is used for the word *under*.

54. The suffix *thing* is expressed by a dot in the following words:

anything ────.   something ───.   everything ╱.

55. Plurals of Brief Forms.

The plurals of brief forms ending in *s* are formed by adding another *s* of the same motion, thus:

cause   causes   business   businesses

In other brief forms the plurals are formed by adding *s* to the singular forms, thus:

parts   changes   ships   forms

56. READING AND DICTATION PRACTICE

UNIT 6

57. The Letter X. When *x* occurs at the end of or within words, it is expressed by *s* slightly modified in slant, thus:

mix	⌁	fix	⌁	tax	ℓ
mixes	⌁	fixes	⌁	taxes	ℛ

NOTE: The plural is formed by adding *s* as shown in *mixes*, *taxes*.

SIMPLE SUFFIXES

58. The suffix *shun* (*sion*, *tion*) is expressed by *sh*:

mention	⟶	fashion	⌁	vision	⌁
nation	⌁	action	⌁	session	⌁
mission	⌁	faction	⌁	evasion	⌁
diction	⌁	affection	⌁	section	⌁

59. The Past Tense. The past tense is expressed by *t* or *d*:

1. After most abbreviated words a disjoined *t* placed close to the preceding character is used to express the past tense, thus:

changed	timed	liked	willed
⌁	⌁	⌁	⌁

2. In all other cases join *t* or *d* if a distinctive and facile joining is possible; otherwise, disjoin *t* (as in g*lared, tapered*) to express the past tense, thus:

passed		raced		shaped	
praised		mentioned		reached	
visited		risked		checked	
labored		glared		tapered	
traced		fixed		feared	

60. BRIEF FORMS FOR COMMON WORDS

also		letter, let		until	
nothing		present, presence		got	
between		big, beg		gave	
another		give, given		next	
woman		tell,* till		soon	
morning		still		name	

*The *s* is added to *tell* by changing the circle into a loop, thus: *tells*

BRIEF FORMS AS PREFIXES

61. A brief form is frequently used as a prefix or as part of another word, as illustrated in the following:

almost	inform	formal
income	begin	anyone
increase	began	overwork
instead	forgive	undergo
ago	forgot	handle

62. FREQUENT PHRASES

for the	you have	would be
to be*	there is	can be
with the	of his	may be
I have	for you	and that
from the	if you	as the
of this	of your	in our
there are	in this	of all

*Before a downstroke, *to* is expressed by *t.*

63. READING AND DICTATION PRACTICE

(shorthand outlines)

64. WRITING PRACTICE

1. I shall not leave here today for my trip to France, as I am too busy, but I shall finish everything soon.

2. It may be that such a change in the history classes will help to settle the matter for you.

3. He will cash the pay check if you will present it at his desk.

4. Since she is changing her plans to stay here some time before going to the city, I think it will be well to leave the matter as it is for the present.

5. Because the business in that part of the country is not good, he will remain there another month to go thoroughly into the planning of a sales campaign.

6. It is plain that if any action is to be taken it must take place before the session ends today.

7. He fixed the time at six and said that the men were asleep.

8. I shall not fail to mention that the basis of his claim is very flimsy and that I feel that his figures should be thoroughly studied and checked before any decision is reached.

Dear Sir: The sale of the goods you shipped me in January is not going at all well. For one thing, the season has been very late, causing business to be slack. Can you think of anything that will help our sales? It may be that business in other parts of the country is much the same as it is here and you have made some sales plans that will be of help to me. I should like to go over this matter with one of your men the first time one of them is in the city. Yours truly,

CHAPTER III

UNIT 7

THE Ō-HOOK

65. The lower half of the elliptical figure θ is called the *o-hook*. It is used to express the following sounds:

ŏ	aw	ō
as in	*as in*	*as in*
rot	raw	wrote
r ŏ t	r aw	r ō t

Key to Vowel Sounds: John   Paul   Jones.

NOTE: The sound *aw* is spelled in various ways, as in *fall*, *bought*, *taught*, *raw*. The same method of marking vowels is employed in this chapter as in the first.

66. FREQUENT-WORD DRILL

know	n ō		lot	l ŏ t	
law	l aw		road	r ō d	
low	l ō		load	l ō d	
wrote	r ō t		ought	aw t	

auto	aw t ō		hope	h ō p	
note	n ō t		show	sh ō	
bought	b aw t		shop	sh ŏ p	
brought	b r aw t		folks	f ō k s	
blow	b l ō		taught	t aw t	
ball	b aw l		caught	k aw t	
box	b ŏ x		coffee	k ŏ f ē	
job	j ŏ b		hog	h ŏ g	
talk	t aw k		occur	ŏ k 'r	
dog	d ŏ g		hotel	h ō t ĕ l	
noted	n ō ted		slow	s l ō	
notes	n ō t s		abroad	a b r aw d	
notice	n ō t ĭ s		broken	b r ō k 'n	
raw	r aw		open	ō p 'n	
loss	l ŏ s		off	ŏ f	
fellow	f ĕ l ō		often	ŏ f 'n	

so	s ō		phone	f ō n	
saw	s aw		notion	n ō shun	
sought	s aw t		motion	m ō shun	
sorry	s ŏ r ĭ		sober	s ō b 'r	
sorrow	s ŏ r ō		close	k l ō z	
soul	s ō l		model	m ŏ d 'l	
soft	s ŏ f t		solemn	s ŏ l ĕ m	
snow	s n ō		solid	s ŏ l ĭ d	

67. O-Hook Modified. To avoid an unnecessary angle, the slant of the *o*-hook is modified slightly before *n*, *m*, *r*, and *l*, thus:

When a downstroke comes before the *o*-hook, this rule does not apply, since the *o*-hook joins to downstrokes without an angle, as in:

pour   shown   bone   pole

68. FREQUENT-WORD DRILL

on	ŏ n		home	h ō m
own	ō n		known	n ō n

or	aw r	⌣	nor	n aw r	⌣
roar	r ō r		omitted	ō m ĭ ted	
roll	r ō l		drawn	d r aw n	
lower	l ō'r		horse	h aw r s	
whole	h ō l		alone	a l ō n	
loan	l ō n		store	s t ō r	
coal	k ō l		story	s t ō r ĭ	
tone	t ō n		college	k ŏ l ĕ j	
door	d ō r		grown	g r ō n	

69. BRIEF FORMS FOR COMMON WORDS

want*	⌐	glad, girl	⌐	call	⌐
went*	⌐	during, Dr.	⌐	situation	⌐
told	⌐	believe, belief	6	course	⌐
order	⌐	possible	6	general	⌐
small	⌐	purpose	⌐	several	⌐
upon	⌐	receive	⌐	state	⌐

*The *w* is omitted in *want* and *went*.

70. READING AND DICTATION PRACTICE

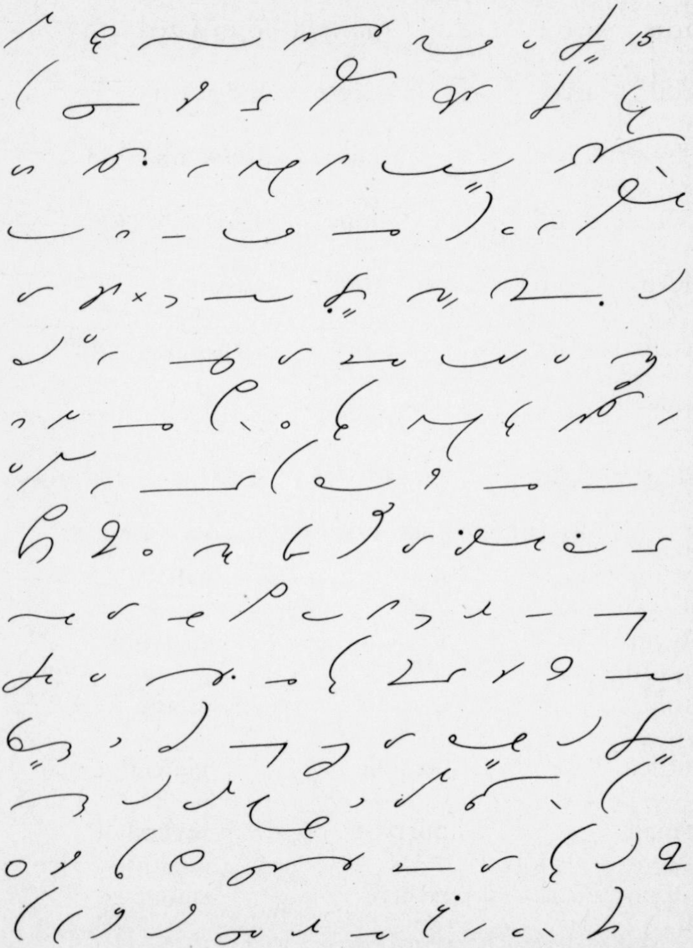

UNIT 8

METHOD OF EXPRESSING R

71. The circle is written with left motion to express *r* following the vowel:

1. Before and after straight strokes:

art   mar   arch   share

2. Between straight strokes in the same direction:

tart   dared   church   murmur

72. It is generally more facile to use the circle for the obscure vowel sound heard in *ur* as in *church*, *murmur*, *urge*, *hurt*.

73. FREQUENT-WORD DRILL

heart		urge		better	
hard		tear		later	
hurt		dare		sister	
heard		near		chapter	
earn		mere		motor	
arm		manner		cashier	
army		chair		minister	
harm		jar		teacher	

S FOLLOWING A LEFT-MOTION CIRCLE

74. The letter *s* is added to a final left-motion circle on straight strokes by changing the circle to a loop:

tears		shares		stairs	
dares		nears		manners	

75. BRIEF FORMS FOR COMMON WORDS

either		deal, dear		yesterday	
above		real, regard		together	
rather		company, keep		children	
love		become, book		prepare	
collect		importance, important		subject	
capital		necessary		opinion	

76. After abbreviated words and words ending in a left-motion circle on straight strokes, a disjoined *r* expresses *er, or*, thus:

keeper		dearer		worker	

When the forms are distinctive, the *r* is joined, thus:

greater		bigger		smaller	

When a brief form ends with the last *consonant* of a word, the left motion circle is used to express *or, er* after straight strokes:

sooner		former	

77. READING AND DICTATION PRACTICE

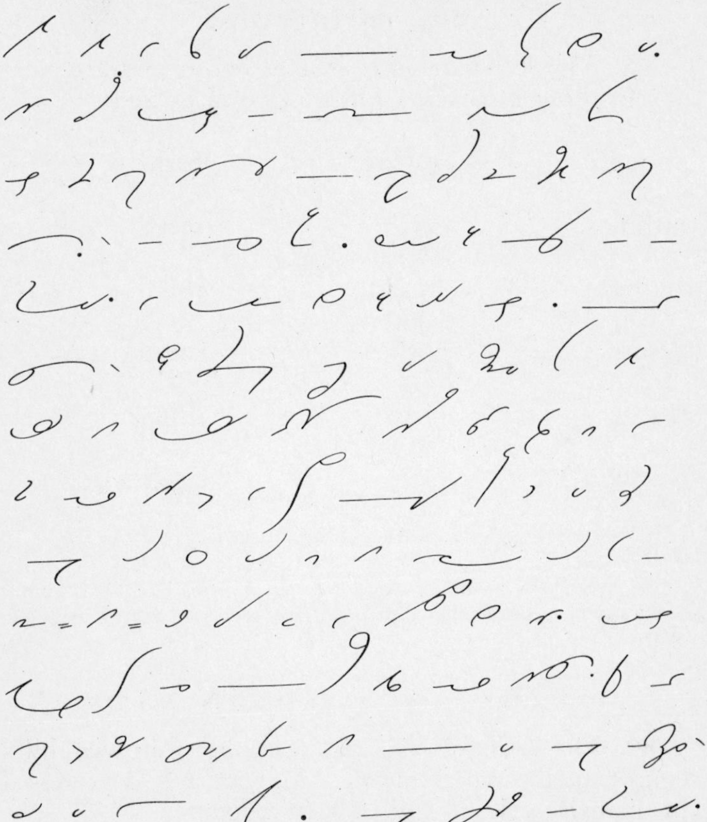

UNIT 9

THE TH JOININGS

78. The left-motion *th* is used before and after *o, r, l.* In other cases the right-motion *th* is used:

though		author		bath	
although*		earth		teeth	
thought		health		thief	
throw		both		theater	
throat		birth		thin	
thrown		path		cloth	

*The word *although* is a combination of *all* and *though.*

79. When *th* is the only consonant stroke, as in the brief forms for *that* or *they*, or is in combination with *s*, the right-motion *th* is used, as in *these* and *seethe*.

FREQUENT PREFIXES AND SUFFIXES

80. The prefixes *con, com, coun, cog,* followed by a consonant, are expressed by *k.* The suffix *ly* is expressed by a small circle; *ily* and *ally,* by a loop:

confess		council		conform	
confer		compel		county	

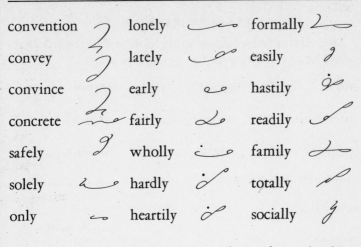

convention		lonely		formally	
convey		lately		easily	
convince		early		hastily	
concrete		fairly		readily	
safely		wholly		family	
solely		hardly		totally	
only		heartily		socially	

81. In words beginning with *comm* or *conn*, the second *m* or *n* is written, thus:

common ⁓⁓⁓   connote ⁓⁓   commence ⁓⁓

When *con* or *com* is followed by a vowel or by *r* or *l*, write *kn* for *con* and *km* for *com*, thus:

comedy ⁓⁓   comrade ⁓⁓   comic ⁓⁓

82. After a circle vowel, *ly* is written on the opposite side from the vowel, thus:

dearly   daily   nearly

83. To express the plural of some brief forms ending in a circle and of some words ending in a loop, a slight change is made in the manner of joining *s*, thus:

names   letters   families

PHRASING PRINCIPLES

84. Before words beginning with a downward character or *o*, *r*, *l*, the word *to* is expressed by *t*:

to see		to say		to pay	
to which		to honor		to work	
to ship		to our		to place	

85. When repeated in a phrase, *as* is expressed by *s*:

as well as		as much as	
as good as		as great as	
as low as		as many as	

86. After *be* or *been*, the word *able* is expressed by *a*:

have been able		should be able	
would be able		will be able	

87. FREQUENT PHRASES

on the		with you		about the	
you are		if the		to give	
must be		as to		you know	
should be		at that		of it	

that is	*9*	of their	*~*	which is	*/*
in which	*7*	is not	*2*	on you-r	*~*
of these	*9*	of which	*9*	with that	*8*
more than	*—*	to get	*~*	from you	*2*
your letter	*~*	to take	*~*	of its	*~*
this is	*9*	in his	*~*	he will	*~*
you may	*~*	if you will	*2*	you would	*~*
he is	*9*	that this	*8*	to this	*~*

88. BRIEF FORMS FOR COMMON WORDS

send	*~*	special, speak, speech	*(*	represent	*~*
agree*	....	week, weak	*~*	already	*~*
ask	*~*	floor, flour	*~*	value	*~*
office	*9*	complete,† complain-t	*7*	employ	*~*
official	*~*	immediate, immediately	*~*	express	*~*
future	*~*	committee	*~*	knowledge	*~*

*The prefix form for *agr-e-i*, a loop written above the following character, is used to express the word *agree*.

†The angle between *k* and *p* is maintained in the word *complete* to make a distinction between *complete* and *keep*.

89. READING AND DICTATION PRACTICE

(shorthand outlines)

90. WRITING PRACTICE

1. It is hard to say what is known about the model of the motor on which Horace Holliday is working. Several people have seen it and praise it.

2. After Bob bought the boat he noticed that the motor would stall often. After much analysis and pottering over it, he spotted the cause of grief. It was a little thing, and easy to fix.

3. The history of this country shows that a hardy, hard-working people, gifted with vision, can achieve what they fix as a goal if the goal has a meaning to the people in general.

4. It was a shock to her to hear that John Jones, after joking about it, really had started alone on an airplane trip to Havana and was nearing his goal.

5. The "Lone Eagle" did not cross the ocean merely by dreaming of it. He made ready for a great trip by planning every detail. Study, hard work, and the bravery to face peril without flinching helped him to achieve his aim and to place his name on the scroll of the great men of history.

Dear Sir: It will be necessary for me to stay here till about the end of January, as there are many matters of importance still to be finished. I am really glad that you were able to see Mr. Hartman and close that business with him. Such matters may easily cause hard feeling. There is nothing at present that needs your presence here. The general situation seems to be as good as it is in the East. I have my heart set on making big gains for the company here this month. I am working hard to achieve all possible. Yours truly,

CHAPTER IV

UNIT 10

THE $\overline{oo}$-HOOK

91. The upper part of the small elliptical figure ⟨⟩ , which is called the *$\overline{oo}$-hook*, is used to express the following sounds:

ŭ	ŏŏ	$\overline{oo}$
as in	*as in*	*as in*
tuck	took	tomb
t ŭ k	t ŏŏ k	t $\overline{oo}$ m

Key to Vowel Sounds:

The   duck   took   to the   pool.

92. FREQUENT-WORD DRILL

who	h $\overline{oo}$		hug	h ŭ g	
do	d $\overline{oo}$.		does	d ŭ z	
took	t ŏŏ k		up	ŭ p	
true	t r $\overline{oo}$		upper	ŭ p 'r	
whom	h $\overline{oo}$ m		blue	b l $\overline{oo}$	

48

plus	p l ŭ s		fruit	f r oo t	
pull	p oo l		roof	r oo f	
lose	l oo z		luck	l ŭ k	
rug	r ŭ g		rub	r ŭ b	
rough	r ŭ f		foot	f oo t	
food	f oo d		shut	sh ŭ t	
fur	f ŭ r		sugar	sh oo g 'r	
supper	s ŭ p 'r		fool	f oo l	
dozen	d ŭ z 'n		tough	t ŭ f	
group	g r oo p		stuff	s t ŭ f	
cut	k ŭ t		truck	t r ŭ k	
cook	k oo k		us	ŭ s	
cup	k ŭ p		thus	th ŭ s	
oven	ŭ v 'n		sullen	s ŭ l ĕ n	
cousin	k ŭ z 'n		through	thr oo	

93. The combination *us* is written without an angle at the beginning of words, or when it follows a downstroke or *k*, *g*, as in *us, shoes, campus, cousin,* etc.

94. The o͞o-hook Modified. To avoid an unnecessary angle, the o͞o-hook is turned under after *n, m*. It is also turned under after *k* or *g* if followed by *r* or *l*:

mood	m o͞o d		canoe	k ă n o͞o	
none	n ŭ n		muff	m ŭ f	
noon	n o͞o n		nook	n ŏ k	
moon	m o͞o n		null	n ŭ l	
nut	n ŭ t		cool	k o͞o l	
numb	n ŭ m		cur	k ŭ r	
annul	ă n ŭ l		curse	k ŭ r s	

95. BRIEF FORMS FOR COMMON WORDS

care		skill, school		number	
carry		usual, wish		enough	
force		govern, -ment		position	
charge		expect, especial		question	
look		full		purchase	
clear		sure		remember	

96. READING AND DICTATION PRACTICE

UNIT 11

METHOD OF EXPRESSING W

97. By pronouncing the following words slowly it will be found that *w* has the sound of $\overline{oo}$; therefore *w* is expressed by the $\overline{oo}$-hook:

we	=	$\overline{oo}$-ē
wave	=	$\overline{oo}$-ā-v
wall	=	$\overline{oo}$-aw-l

98. WORD DRILL

way	w ā		win	w ĭ n	
wet	w ĕ t		wane	w ā n	
wait	w ā t		women	w ĭ men	
weighed	w ā d		wake	w ā k	
wed	w ĕ d		wicked	w ĭ k ĕ d	
wedded	w ĕ ded		walk	w aw k	
width	w ĭ d th		weave	w ē v	
widow	w ĭ d ō		waste	w ā s t	

wash	w ŏ sh		weep	w ē p	
watch	w ŏ ch		web	w ĕ b	
wages	w ā j 's		wheat*	hw ē t	
wedge	w ĕ j		wheel	hw ē l	
wear	w ā r		whim	hw ĭ m	
weary	w ē r ĭ		whip	hw ĭ p	
wool	w o͞o l		whale	hw ā l	
water	w aw ter		whirl	hw ĕ r l	

*In the combination *wh*, as in *wheel*, the *h* is sounded first.

99. W Within Words. In the body of a word it is more convenient to express *w* by a dash placed beneath the vowel following. In writing *sw* and a circle vowel, as in *sweet*, *swim*, *swell*, the hook for *w* is preferable to the dash:

quick		equity		squall	
queen		queer		swim	
quit		twin		swell	
quote		dwell		swift	
acquit		sweet		doorway	

100. A Before W or H. In words beginning with *a-h* or *a-w* the dot, placed on the line close to the next character, is used to express *a*:

ahead		awake		await	
away		awoke		awaken	

101. FREQUENT PHRASES

we are		we are not		we shall be	
we will		we will not		we have	
we shall		we shall not		we have been	
we can		we cannot		we have not	

102. BRIEF FORMS FOR COMMON WORDS

world		house, whose		suppose	
reply		remark, room		whether	
word		follow, fall		further	
body		accept, -ance		explain	
duty		gone		particular	
bring		nature		report	

103. READING AND DICTATION PRACTICE

[Gregg shorthand outlines]

UNIT 12

METHOD OF EXPRESSING Y

104. Y has the sound of long *e*, as in *yacht*, *yoke*, and when followed by a hook vowel is expressed by the small circle.   *Ye*, as in *year*, *yet*, is expressed by a small loop; *ya*, by a large loop.

yacht		yellow		youth	
yawn		yoke		yarn	
year		yet		yard	

THE SIGNS FOR NG AND NK

105. The sound *ng*, as in *ring*, *rang*, is expressed by *n* written at a slightly downward slant; *nk* (sounded *ngk*), as in *bank*, *rank*, is expressed by a longer stroke on the same slant:

ring		drink		bank	
rang		sank		blank	
rank		wing		king	
sing		frank		wrong	
songs		banquet		spring	

PREFIXES AND SUFFIXES

106. The vowel is omitted in the prefixes *en, in, un, em, im* when the prefix is followed by a consonant; when a written vowel follows the prefix, the initial vowel is retained. *Ex* is expressed by *es*.

The suffix *ings* is expressed by a left *s* and *ingly* by a small circle substituted for the *ing*-dot:

infer		unseen		expense	
envy		engine		lovingly	
impel		innate		seem-ingly	
impres-sion		emotion		exceed-ingly	
embrace		emit		meetings	
emphasis		examine		savings	
indeed		excess		evenings	

107. Negative words beginning with *in, un, im* in which the *n* or *m* is doubled are distinguished from the positive forms by omitting one of the doubled consonants and inserting the initial vowel:

known		unknown	
noticed		unnoticed	
necessary		unnecessary	

108. FREQUENT PHRASES

of them		to ask		if you are	
very much		we would		are not	
when the		we should		we may	
at all		does not		with us	
into the		we must		will you	
in reply		that they		through the	
on our		to keep		for us	
to go		which have		over the	
did not		who have		as you	

109. BRIEF FORMS FOR COMMON WORDS

long		strength, strong		character	
among		communi-cate,-tion		effect	
young		bill, built		return	
yes		friend, friendly		answer	
thank		else, list		experience	
effort		car, correct		recent	

110. READING AND DICTATION PRACTICE

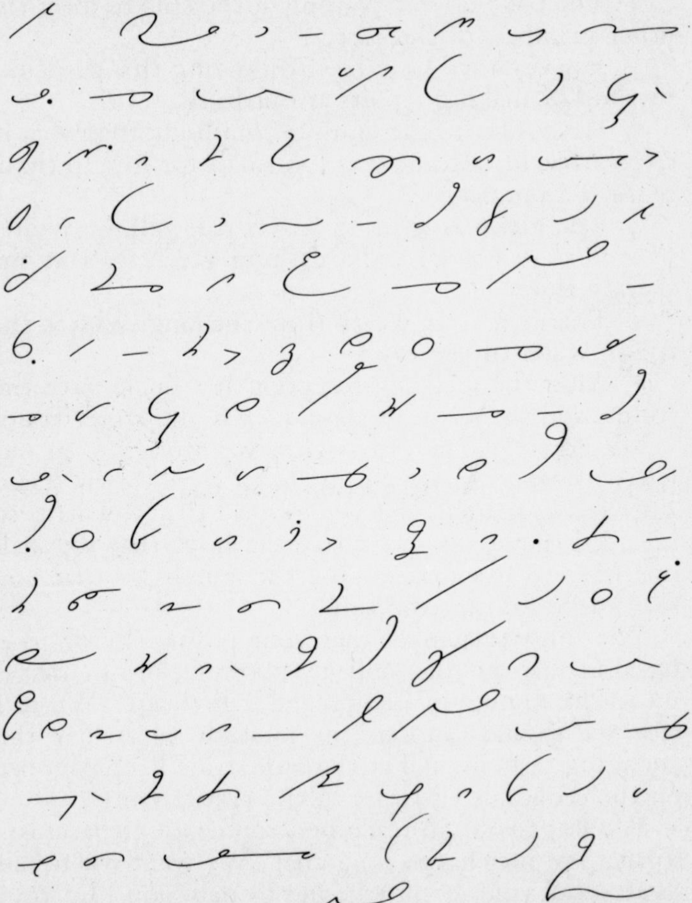

111. WRITING PRACTICE

1. The couple were waiting at the club to meet the other members of the party.

2. For years we have been following this particular method of making reports at our bank.

3. His answer to the unusual communication was, in effect, that his income was too small for him to think of such a purchase.

4. The girl was wearing a new pale yellow sweater of soft angora wool and a dashing green scarf at the skating rink.

5. The men were weary from the long swim in the rough water of the bay.

6. After the wedding reception her uncle gave the couple and their friends a banquet at the Hotel Tours.

My dear Sir: The orders that we gave you in our letter of May 1 about all purchases were clearly stated and very important, and we are glad that you have so regarded them.   In the future we hope that we shall not have to question any of the purchases that you may make for our company.

You must remember that your position with us is based mainly on your skill in choosing clothing that is up to the minute in fashion and still cheap.   We feel that we should caution you to study every day the changing fashions and at the same time keep your eye on the economic situation in the textile world.

We hope you can reach here soon enough Saturday, so that we may have a long chat.   We want you to tell us all about your recent trip and to help you plan your next trip to Paris.   Yours truly,

CHAPTER V

UNIT 13

THE DIPHTHONGS

112. A pure diphthong is the union in one syllable of two simple vowel sounds uttered in rapid succession. The diphthongs are therefore expressed by joining the circles and hooks representing the vowel sounds of which the diphthongs are composed:

ū	𝒐	*as in* fume	f ū m	𝆑	
ow	𝒐	*as in* now	n ow	⟋	
oi	𝒐	*as in* oil	oi l	ℓ	
ī	𝒪	*as in* die	d ī	℘	

NOTE: The diphthong *u* is a combination of *ē* and *ōo*; *ow*, of *ä* and *ōo*; *oi*, of *aw* and *ē*. The sign for the diphthong *i* is a large circle with an indentation—resembling a combination of *ä* and *ē*, which, if uttered in rapid succession, yield a sound almost equivalent to *ī*. This sign is generally called "the broken circle."

The signs are written in their *sounded* order. The sign for the diphthong *i* is treated as a circle, and conforms to the rules for joining circles. Note how the diphthong *i* is written in the words *size, nice, price, mine,* which appear in the following word drill.

113. WORD DRILL

human		enjoy		white	
cute		join		wise	
few		boy		wide	
view		toy		ride	
now		voice		lie	
cow		high		price	
mouth		size		prices	
ounce		rise		prize	
vow		fight		apply	
bough		fine		supply	
annoy		file		comply	
noise		sign		cry	
oil		fire		nice	
soil		fly		mine	
choice		sight		realize	

type		try		dining	
pipe		tried		twice	
final		dry		excited	
smile*		drive		tie	
died		design		tire	

*See *mile* in the brief forms below.

114. For convenience, long *i* is expressed by the large circle in the following words:

life   line   quite   might

115. BRIEF FORMS FOR COMMON WORDS

use		how, out		side	
power		right, write		wire	
why		while		kind	
night		behind		inquire	
find		point, appoint		mile	
light		thousand		require	

116. When word forms end with the diphthong *i*, the double circle is used to express the diphthong and the termination *ly*:

lightly   kindly   rightly   nightly

117. READING AND DICTATION PRACTICE

UNIT 14

OTHER VOWEL COMBINATIONS

118. In a few words, vowels follow one another consecutively without forming diphthongs, as in *poem*, *radio*, *showy*. In such words the signs for the sounds are written in the order in which the sounds occur:

poet		snowy*		radio	
poem		showy		folio	

*When necessary, the long sound of *o* in *oe* is marked to distinguish it from the diphthong *oi*.

119. Any vowel following the diphthong *i* is expressed by a small circle within the large circle:

via		science		riot	
fiat		diet		prior	

120. Short *i* followed by *a*, as in *mania*, is expressed by a large circle with a dot placed within it; *e* followed by the large circle vowel, as in *create*, is expressed by a large circle with a dash within it. These distinctions are seldom necessary, however:

aria		cereal		piano	
area		serial		create	
alias		mania		creation	

OMISSION OF MINOR VOWELS

121. When two vowels not forming a pure diphthong come together, the minor vowel may be omitted. For convenience in writing many common words, the circle may be omitted in the diphthong *u*, as in *new, due, music*:

theory	due	idea*
genius	music	ideal*
arduous	amuse	genuine
tedious	reduce	renew
new	avenue	renewal

*The long *i* in *idea* and *ideal* is expressed by the large circle.

122. BRIEF FORMS FOR COMMON WORDS

dollar*	respect, respectful-ly	please
object	arrange, arrangement	progress
strange	consider, consideration	across
trust	opportunity	various
mail	throughout	enclose
address	advantage	wonder

*After numerals, *dollars* is expressed by *d*.

123. READING AND DICTATION PRACTICE

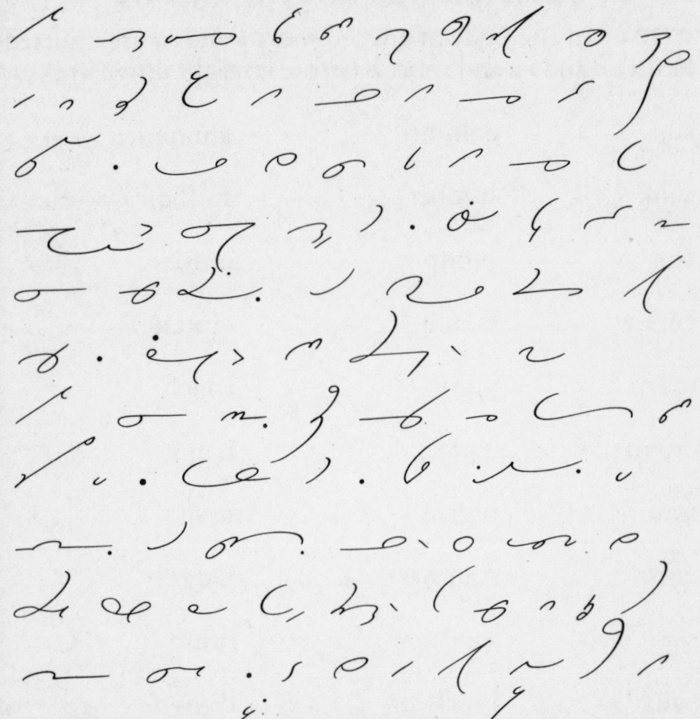

UNIT 15

OMISSION OF SHORT U AND OW

124. In the body of a word short *u* and *ow* are omitted before *n* and *m*, and short *u* before straight downstrokes:

sun	column	announce
sunk	lumber	million
fun	pump	crush
funny	bunch	clutch
town	jump	touch
down	brown	trunk
ton	begun	rush
done	summer	judge
run	sunshine	brush
rung	luncheon	drown

125. Between *n-n*, *ow* is indicated by a jog, as in *announce*; short *u* is inserted between *n-n*, *n-m*, as in *nun* and *numb*; *moun* is expressed by the *men* blend, as in *mountain*.

126. The *u* is omitted in the termination *sume*:

assume	resume	consume	presume

JOINED PREFIXES AND SUFFIXES

127. The syllables *per, pro, pur* are expressed by *pr*; the syllable *ble*, by *b*; *ple*, by *p* (in the words given below only); *ment*, by *m*:

proper		trouble		sample	
process		sensible		example	
perhaps		miser- able		apart- ment	
permit		suitable		compli- ment	
promo- tion		avail- able		moment	
pursue		terrible		equip- ment	
promise		reliable		treat- ment	
prove		noble		element	
perform		payable		excite- ment	
profit		simple		payment	
valuable		ample		settle- ment	

128. When *pro* occurs before an upward character or *k*, it is more convenient to insert the vowel, as in:

protection   produce   produced

COMPOUND JOINED PREFIXES

129. Two or more simple prefixes may be joined:

inform		unexpected*	
conform		uncomfortable	
reconcile		unaccountable*	
recognize		uninformed	
unforeseen		unemployed	
unexplored*		incomplete	
unimportant		unconscious	

*The initial vowel is not required in compound prefixes.

130. BRIEF FORMS FOR COMMON WORDS

problem		person, personal		perfect, proof	
success		regret, regular		satisfy, -factory	
probable		confident, confidence		bed, bad	
except		correspond, -ence		cover	
stop		excel-lent, excellence		serious	
accord		organize, organization		direct	

131. READING AND DICTATION PRACTICE

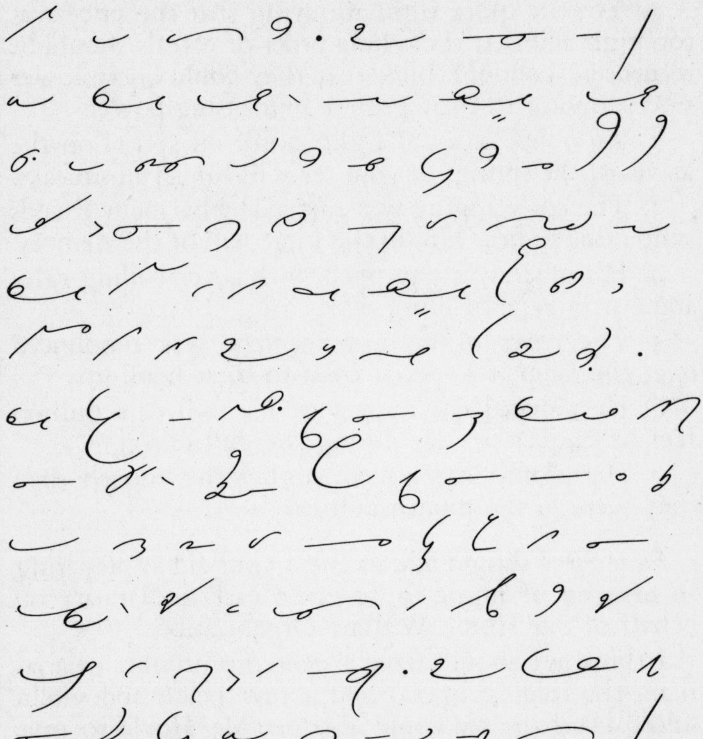

132. WRITING PRACTICE

1. You are quite right in saying that the price was too high and that the whole order of cereals should be returned. I should think that they could quote lower prices, owing to their greater purchasing power.

2. An ounce or so of light motor oil spread on the leaves of the springs of your car will banish all squeaks.

3. The boy's singing was enjoyed by his many friends who came to hear him in the huge hall of the Armory.

4. His office was equipped with several filing cases and a new type of filing desk.

5. The news of his appointment was announced over the radio at a special coast-to-coast hook-up.

6. He reduced the output of his mill to a million feet of lumber per day during the dull season.

7. His profits in oil were higher this month than they were in the month before.

Dear Sir: I should like to enlist your aid in preparing an evening of music to be given early in January on behalf of our Home Welfare Organization.

I think we should have a generous number of arias from the leading operas and a few piano and violin solos. Perhaps we could also get Mr. Hoyle to give his talk on the poetry of music. We must not forget also to present some numbers for the enjoyment of the children who will be present.

Will you not join with us in helping to arrange something of an unusually high character this year? Yours truly,

CHAPTER VI

UNIT 16

BLENDED CONSONANTS

133. When two straight lines form an obtuse or blunt angle, the natural tendency of the hand is to "slur" the angle and allow the lines to form a curve, thus:

blended becomes and expresses *-nt, -nd*

blended becomes and expresses *-mt, -md*

134. The *-nt, -nd* blend is an *upward* curve, corresponding in length to the sign for *f*; the *-mt, -md* blend is an *upward* curve, corresponding in length to *v*. The *n* or *m* governs the length of the curve; the curve containing *m* naturally is longer. At the beginning of words, short *e* and short *i* are omitted before these blends, as in *entry, empty, induce*, etc.

135. WORD DRILL

bond	band	prevent
print	prompt	owned
planned	blind	rent
plenty	apparent	land

73

around		seemed		grant	
entry		second		convent	
Indian		fastened		ground	
empty		signed		trimmed	
refund		event		strained	
laundry		front		winter	
joint		framed		inventory	
sound		exempt		moaned	
found		count		doomed	
sent		gained		ashamed	

136. The Ld Combination. The combination *ld* is expressed by giving *l* a swinging upward turn at the finish:

old		fold		gold	
older		field		killed	
yield		failed		filed	
held		wild		child	

hold	cold	sealed
sold	colder	appealed

137. DAYS AND MONTHS

Sunday	January	August
Monday	February	September
Tuesday	March	October
Wednesday	April	November
Thursday	May	December
Friday	June	
Saturday	July	

138. BRIEF FORMS FOR COMMON WORDS

entire	refer, reference	receipt
copy	remit, remittance	unable
stock	suggest, suggestion	enable
stand	individual	invoice
allow	attention	industry
draft	acknowledge	oblige

139. READING AND DICTATION PRACTICE

UNIT 17

JENT-PENT, DEF-TIVE BLENDS

140. By rounding off the angle, as shown in the previous blends, the following useful signs for syllables are obtained:

blended becomes ⟍ and expresses *jent-d, pent-d*

blended becomes ⟍ and expresses *def-v, -tive*

141. WORD DRILL

spend		cheapened		defeat	
expend		carpenter		defer	
happened		pageant		defy	
opened		impending		divine	
cogent		native		deficit	
legend		devout		division	
ripened		divided		device	
gentle		defraud		defend	
genteel		defray		defense	
Gentile		endeavor		define	

sensitive		positive		motive	
restive		creative		captive	

142. SPECIAL BUSINESS FORMS

Gentlemen		Yours very sincerely	
Dear Mr.		Yours respectfully	
Messrs.		Respectfully yours	
Yours sincerely		Very respectfully	
Sincerely yours		Cordially yours	
Very sincerely		Yours cordially	

143. BRIEF FORMS FOR COMMON WORDS

move		differ-ent, difference		quality	
agent		approximate		definite	
spirit		deliver, delivery		tomorrow	
credit		instant, instance		influence	
appear		response, responsible		mistake-n	
beauty		railway, rule		altogether	

144. READING AND DICTATION PRACTICE

(shorthand outlines)

UNIT 18

FREQUENT WORD-BEGINNINGS

145. The vowel is omitted in the syllables *be, de, re, dis,* and *mis:*

below	discover	reason
beneath	dispel	reasonable
besides	dispatch	reception
delay	display	review
debate	dislike	revise
deceit	disgrace	replace
decision	dismiss	repent
depress	repair	mislaid
depart	resign	mishap
depend	reform	misery

146. The vowel is retained when *de* precedes *k, g,* as in *decay, degrade.*

147. The vowel in *re* is omitted only before a downward character, as in *replace, repent, review, repair, resign, reception.*

PHRASING PRINCIPLES

148. The word *had* when following a pronoun is expressed as shown in the following illustrations:

I had	he had	they had	we had	you had

149. The phrases *was-not* and *is-not* are expressed easily and legibly by using the blending principle:

was not   he was not   it is not

it was not   there was not   there is not

NOTE: If the contractions *wasn't*, *isn't*, etc. need to be positively indicated, the apostrophe is placed above the forms.

150. BRIEF FORMS FOR COMMON WORDS

record	improve, -ment	newspaper, inspect
advertise	acquaint, -ance	sufficient
previous	nevertheless, envelope	merchan- dise
occasion	insure, insurance	determine
quantity	educate, education	pleasure
hundred	difficult, difficulty	catalogue

151. READING AND DICTATION PRACTICE

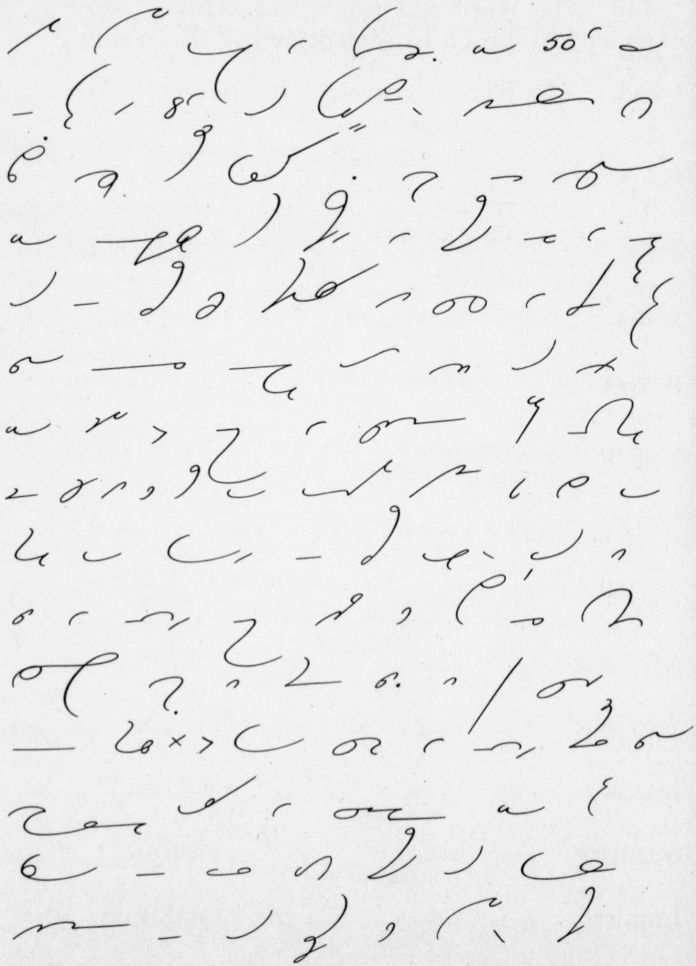

152. WRITING PRACTICE

1. Apparently, this new house is endeavoring to underwrite the entire issue of the ship-canal bonds without calling upon any of the stronger and better-known houses.

2. Were you present yesterday evening at the reception to the new minister from France?

3. We have failed to find in the inventory any record of the number of batteries on hand December 31.

4. They discovered that the dispatch had not been delivered until after the stock market had opened.

5. The factory promptly made the consignee a satisfactory refund on the carload of goods.

6. It would be easier to replace those old buildings than to repair them.

7. I want you to change your window display every other day after closing hours.

8. The collection agency moved cautiously in the matter of collecting the old accounts that had been referred to it by the Retail Dealers' organization.

9. The Committee will hold its second session at the White House tomorrow morning.

Dear Madam: In the hope that we may be of some help to you in completing your shopping list for the summer season, we wish to call your attention to our mesh bags. Our complete line gives you a wealth of unusually pretty styles at very reasonable prices.

A visit to our Jewelry Department to look at these bags will prove profitable to you. Very truly yours,

CHAPTER VII

UNIT 19

TEN-DEN, TEM-DEM BLENDS

153. By blending *t* or *d* with *n* or *m* facile blends result, which make possible the writing of many syllables with but one movement of the pen:

blended becomes ⟋ and expresses *ten, den*

blended becomes ⟋ and expresses *tem, dem*

154. WORD DRILL

sudden	continue	broaden
written	continued	danger
threaten	continues	tender
hidden	continuous	denote
extension	intention	dinner
evidence	deny	tonight
sentence	distance	tennis
condense	residence	contain

84

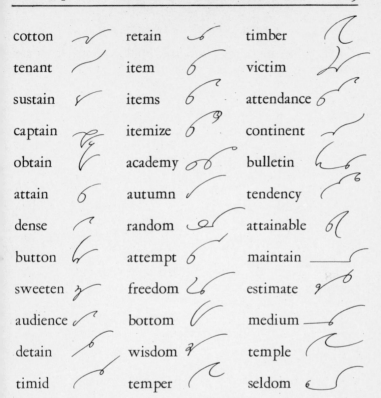

cotton	retain	timber
tenant	item	victim
sustain	items	attendance
captain	itemize	continent
obtain	academy	bulletin
attain	autumn	tendency
dense	random	attainable
button	attempt	maintain
sweeten	freedom	estimate
audience	bottom	medium
detain	wisdom	temple
timid	temper	seldom

155. The blend is not employed when a strongly accented vowel or diphthong occurs in the syllable. Such words as *dean*, *dine*, *team*, *tame*, *dome*, *dime*, and other words of one syllable are written in full. The syllable *tain*, as in *maintain*, *attain*, however, is expressed by *ten*.

156. Where it is possible to use either *ten-den* or *ent-end*, as in *intention*, the right-motion blend is given preference.

PHRASING PRINCIPLES

157. The blending principle makes possible some interesting and valuable phrases:

to me	to make	at any time
to my	at once	in due course
to meet	it must be	in due time
to mean	it may be	what to do
to know	at any	to draw

158. When *do-not* is preceded by a pronoun, it is expressed by the sign *den*:

I do not	we do not believe
I do not see	they do not
I do not know	they do not know
I do not believe	you do not
we do not	you do not know

159. When necessary, *don't* may be distinguished from *do not* by writing *don* for *don't*, thus:

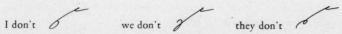

I don't   we don't   they don't

160. READING AND DICTATION PRACTICE

UNIT 20

METHOD OF EXPRESSING R

161. A circle or loop is written with the left motion to express *r* following the vowel:

Between a downward character, *(( )) / / /*

and a forward straight stroke, *◝ ◝ _ —* ; compare the following forms:

Right-motion: chat *ʄ*   sham *ơ*   bin *ʆ*   fame *⟩*

Left-motion: chart *ƙ*   charm *ƙ*   burn *Ϭ*   farm *ʓ*

NOTE: The circle is placed *above* the next stroke after *p*, *b*, as in *burn*, *bird*, and below the next stroke in all others, as in *charm*, *farm*.

There is a tendency in rapid writing to curve a straight line when it is followed by a circle. Therefore the distinctive method of joining the circle when it is written with left motion after straight strokes is adopted to prevent any possibility of misreading. Compare *germ* and *bird* in the following drill:

162. WORD DRILL

barn	*Ϭ*	spurt	*Ϭ*	cheered	*ƙ*
bird	*Ϭ*	spared	*Ϭ*	shared	*ƙ*
period	*Ϭ*	experts	*Ϭ*	repaired	*Ϭ*
barter	*Ϭ*	shirt	*ʄ*	chairman	*Ϭ*
burner	*Ϭ*	charter	*ƙ*	germ	*Ϭ*

convert		farmer		varnish	
avert		farmers		pertain	
adjourn		fern		burden	
adjourned		fertile		pertinent	

163. Between a horizontal and an upward stroke the circle is turned with a left motion on the upward stroke to express *r* following the vowel:

cart		courtesy		guarantee	
card		courteous		girder	
curt		mart		smart	
guard		merit		lard	
guard-ian		skirt		flirt	
garden		inert		alert	

164. Before straight lines, *s* in *ser, cer, sar,* and *th* in *ther, thir,* may be written contrary to the usual method of joining to express *r*:

desert		concert		insert	
discern		concern		inserted	

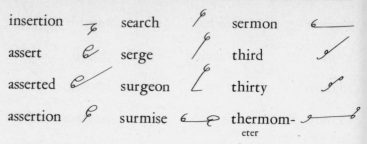

insertion		search		sermon	
assert		serge		third	
asserted		surgeon		thirty	
assertion		surmise		thermom- eter	

165. R Omitted. In many words containing *ar, er, or, ir,* as in the words *large, serve, warm, sort, firm, circle, corner,* the *r* is omitted.

In applying this principle advantage is simply taken of dropping a sound that ordinarily is not stressed in speaking.

166. WORD DRILL

large		reverse		endorse	
larger		reserve		surprise	
learn		toward		surplus	
turn		towards		orchestra	
terms		sport		quarter	
north		born		war	
northern		board		warn	
cord		border		warmth	

warrant		court		western	
serve		source		modern*	
service		storm		southern	
services		firm		assortment	
surface		circle		nervous	
sort		certain		worry	
corn		ascertain		worth	
corner		eastern*		worthy	

*The syllables *tern*, *dern* are expressed by *ten*.

167. The termination *worthy*, as in *noteworthy*, *trustworthy*, is expressed by *thī*, and *worth* by *ŭth*, thus:

noteworthy　　　trustworthy　　　Ainsworth

168. **The Syllable Ther.** The syllable *ther*, as in *either*, *other*, is conveniently expressed by the sign for *th*:

mother		bother		father*	
neither		brother		leather	
gather		weather		hitherto	

*The left-motion *th* is used in *father* to distinguish this word from *faith*, which otherwise would have the same form.

169. READING AND DICTATION PRACTICE

UNIT 21

COMMON PREFIXES AND SUFFIXES

170. The prefixes *for, fore, fur* are expressed by *f*. The suffixes *ful* and *ify* are expressed by *f*; *self* by *s*; *selves* by *ses*; and *age* by *j*:

forget		useful		itself	
forgive		notify		themselves	
forgotten		modify		ourselves	
foresee		certify		yourselves	
furniture		dignify		courage	
furnish		simplify		storage	
awful		myself		baggage	
wonderful		yourself		manager	
helpful		himself		average	
thoughtful		herself		package	

NOTES: (1) The syllable *ture* is written *tr*. (2) The vowel in *baggage* is omitted to distinguish the form from *package*. (3) When *for* or *fore* is followed by a vowel, disjoin *f* close to the next character, as in *forearm*. When *for* or *fore* is followed by *r* or *l*, form an angle after *f*, as in *forerunner, furlong*.

PHRASING PRINCIPLES

171. In phrases, the words *ago, early, few, him, hope, sorry, want, sure, possible,* are modified as shown below:

to *him*		at an early date	
I told him		days *ago*	
we told him		weeks ago	
I *hope*		months ago	
we hope		years ago	
I hope to hear		day or two ago	
I am *sorry*		week or two ago	
we are sorry		as near as *possible*	
I *want*		*few* days	
you want		few months	
we want		few minutes	
if you want		be *sure*	
do you want		we are sure	
early reply		I am sure	

172. READING AND DICTATION PRACTICE

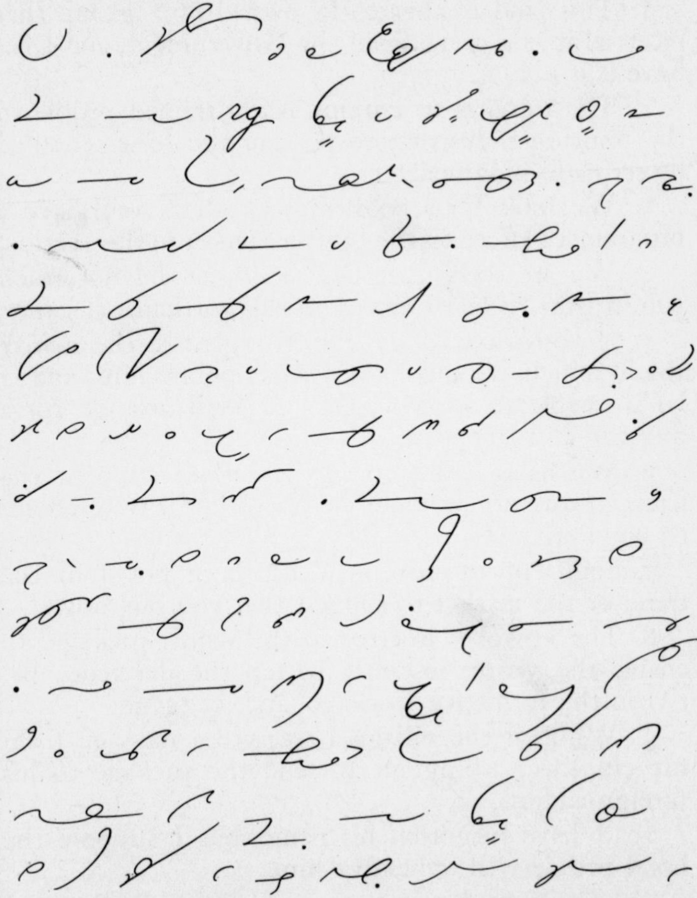

173. WRITING PRACTICE

1. This land is apparently owned by a group that received it as a grant from the Government, and I believe it is tax exempt.

2. The trend is to employ better-trained people in the printing industries, to prevent the losses entailed by errors in judgment.

3. We look for a cold winter, which will have a pronounced effect on the lumber market in this section.

4. We are sorry that the catalogue did not reach you in time to be of service in this particular instance.

5. If you want to see him in regard to the matter about which we talked yesterday, phone him, and if he is unable to see you, then he will arrange for a meeting at a later date.

6. We have looked over the carbon copy of the letter in question and are unable to find any reference to previous prices.

7. Sufficient improvement has been noted in the trend of the market to suggest that you buy now.

8. The vowel is inserted in the word "package" to enable the writer instantly to tell the difference between the forms for "package" and "baggage."

9. While at the village, I received a message from my employer asking me to send the package to his foreign address.

10. I have forgotten his name, but I suppose the hotel people will remember him.

11. The paper has been properly signed by the joint owners and sent to the land office.

CHAPTER VIII

UNIT 22

OMISSION OF FINAL T

174. When slightly enunciated, *t* is omitted at the end of many words.

WORD DRILL

(*t* omitted after *s*)

best		largest		adjust	
rest		modest		adjustment	
west		hardest		disgust	
test		earnest		insist	
latest		honest		consist	
contest		request		persist	
protest		finest		resist	
detest		past		exist	
invest		last		artist	
oldest		just		exhaust	
forest		justice		cost	

175. WORD DRILL
(*t* omitted after *k*, *p*, *den*)

act		project		induct	
enact		affect		adapt	
fact		defect		adopt	
exact		detect		abrupt	
contact		strict		president	
elect		conduct		evident	
select		product		resident	
erect		deduct		student	

176. WORD DRILL
(*t* is written in the following words)

lost		dust		worst	
east		taste		distant	
fast		missed		intent	
cast		mixed		content	
vast		post		extent	
least		coast		patent	

177. READING AND DICTATION PRACTICE

(shorthand outlines)

UNIT 23

OMISSION OF D

178. When slightly enunciated, *d* is often omitted:

mind	dividend	expound
remind	intend	compound
command	extend	compounds
demand	extends	abound
diamond	pound	beyond

179. The *d* is written in the following words:

commend   contend   attend

180. *D* is omitted when it immediately precedes *m* or *v*:

admit	admir- able	admon- ish
admit- tance	advent	adverb
admitted	adventure	admire
advocate	adverse	advance
admira- tion	adversary	advise(ce)

181. In the words *admire, advice, advise, advance,* coming under this rule the initial vowel also is omitted to facilitate phrasing, as illustrated in the

following useful phrases:

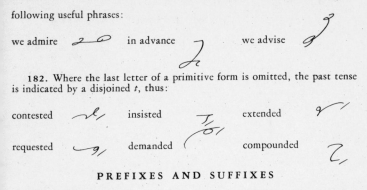

we admire   in advance   we advise

182. Where the last letter of a primitive form is omitted, the past tense is indicated by a disjoined *t*, thus:

contested   insisted   extended

requested   demanded   compounded

PREFIXES AND SUFFIXES

183. The syllable *ul* is expressed by the $\overline{oo}$-hook; *al* (pronounced *aw-l*), by the $\overline{o}$-hook. The sign *al* has already been given in the words *also, almost*. *Sub* is expressed by a joined *s*; *less*, by *l*:

ulster   alterna-   subway
           tive

ultima-   submit   thought-
tum   less

almanac   substance   home-
                         less

alternate*   subside   needless

*For convenience, the root form of the word *alter* is retained in derivative forms, although the pronunciation changes.

184. Before *r, l, ch, j,* or a hook, *s* is written contrary to rule to express *sub*, as in *suburb, sublime, subchief, subjoin*.

185. When *sub* is followed by a circle vowel, *s* is disjoined and placed on the line close to the following character, thus:

subeditor   subhead

186. BRIEF-FORM DERIVATIVE DRILL

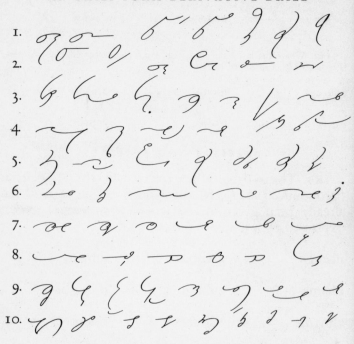

187. KEY TO BRIEF-FORM DRILL

1. acceptable, acknowledgment, addressed, addressee, advantageous, advisable, agreeable; 2. agreement, agreed, answers, appearance, appointment, asked; 3. beautiful, booklet, bookkeeping, careful, causes, charged, clearly; 4. collectible, considerably, correspondent, credits, desirous, educational; 5. effective, enclosure, explanation, favorable, favorite, favors, forced; 6. formerly, fully, greater, greatly, goodness, houses; 7. kindness, kindest, kindly, letters, likely, longer; 8. longest, mostly, myself, namely, names, obligations; 9. occasionally, preparation, publisher, purchaser, qualities, recovered, regardless, regards; 10. representative, satisfactorily, necessarily, necessity, successfully, surely, usually, unusual, wished.

188. READING AND DICTATION PRACTICE

UNIT 24

PHRASING PRINCIPLES

189. Words Omitted. Any unimportant word may be omitted where the sense requires its restoration in transcribing:

in the world		here and there	
ought to be		ought to have	
day or two		ought to receive	
more or less		in reply to your	
little or no		for the time being	
one or two		question of time	
week or two		out of the question	
son-in-law		one of the most	
one of our		sooner or later	
in order to see		in a week or two	
some of them		in reference to the matter	
some of those		in regard to the matter	

up to the time   glad to see

by the way   I am of the opinion

on the market   in such a manner

on the subject   kindly let us know

on the question   in order to prepare

in the matter   little or nothing

in the market   one of the best

hand in hand   in a day or two

that is to say   on account of the way

able to say   I should like to have

more and more   I should like to know

NOTES: 1. To secure facility in execution, split up long phrases and practice progressively, as, for example, *I should, I should like, I should like to know.*

2. The use of such expressions as *in reply to your, for the time being, in regard to the matter,* etc. is to be discouraged. They are not sanctioned by careful writers of English. Nevertheless they are still widely in use in business correspondence, and to prepare students for the kind of dictation they will receive, it is necessary to draw attention to these phrases.

190. READING AND DICTATION PRACTICE

191. WRITING PRACTICE

1. We feel that the extension of the project will not in any way affect the operating costs.

2. The demand for the compound is beyond our power to handle, as the supply of raw products is very limited.

3. I admit that we must admire the way in which he managed his company through a desperate period in its history.

4. We shall attempt to adjust the price of the product to the figure you name, but it is evident that the existing cost of raw products will make this very difficult.

5. Just how the act will affect the sales is hard to predict, but I am almost sure that an adjustment is necessary. The worst feature of the arrangement for the extension of the coast line is that it will greatly reduce, if not exhaust, our present surplus.

6. It is evident from your latest request that you are against the extension of the bond issue, but it is hoped that as a student of finance you will realize that the extension of our operating capital is consistent with modern methods.

7. Stocks and bonds are the two forms of investment most often chosen by the young man or young woman who has heeded the saying we have all heard nearly every day since we were born, that is, "The wise man spends less than he receives."

8. Therefore, when you are ready to start investing, it is much the best plan to rely on an investment bank to recommend the type of investment exactly suited to your needs. It will save you a lot of worry and will cost you nothing.

CHAPTER IX

UNIT 25

THE ABBREVIATING PRINCIPLE

192. The application of the abbreviating principle discussed in Chapter I, paragraph 23, many illustrations of which previously have been given, is more or less flexible and depends to a large extent upon the familiarity of the writer with the words and subject matter in the dictation. Note how the principle is applied in the following illustration:

It is *possible* that the *success* of the *magazine* may

make it *necessary* to change the *policy* of the *association*

at the next meeting in *Phila*delphia sometime in *January.*

Have you a *memo*randum of their *financ*ial standing?

The *February number* will contain an *original* story.

The abbreviating principle is not employed when advantage may be taken of analogical or definite word-building rules, and it should not be employed when easily written word forms are possible without it. A good rule to apply to any word is: When in doubt, write it out.

193. Short Words. In a small but useful group of common words—many illustrations of which have been given throughout this manual in "Brief Forms for Common Words"—the form stops with a diphthong or a strongly accented vowel:

arri(ve)		lou(d)		li(ght)	
deri(ve)		sou(th)		pri(vate)	
enga(ge)		poo(r)		glo(ry)	
stri(ke)		pu(re)		invi(te)	
gra(de)		cu(re)		provi(de)	
tra(de)		pecu(liar)		procee(d)	
dou(bt)		confu(se)		deci(de)	
crow(d)		excu(se)		preva(il)	
prou(d)		refu(se)		repe(at)	
stoo(d)		beca(me)		opera(te)	

194. Long Words. An analysis of hundreds of words shows that the abbreviations of long words fall into three classes, from which the following rules have been established:

195. If there is a longhand abbreviation, it is generally used, if it furnishes a distinctive outline, as in the words *amount (amt.), April (Apr.), balance (bal.), memorandum (memo.)*:

amount (amt.)		R.R.	
balance (bal.)		O.K.	
boulevard (blvd.)		free on board (f.o.b.)	
discount (dis.)		paid (pd.)	
magazine (mag.)		Street* (St.)	
England (Eng.)		horse power (h.p.)	
memorandum* (memo.)		U. S.	
post office (P.O.)		U. S. A.	
equivalent (equiv.)		ultimo (ult.)	
America (Am.)		etc.	

*Memoranda is written *mema; street* is written *st* only with a street name, otherwise *str.*

196. Write through the accented syllable if the outline is distinctive. Illustrations: *abbrev* for *abbreviate*;
lang for *language*; *elab* for *elaborate*, etc.:

authent(ic)

cap(able)

certif(icate)

conven(ience),
conven(ient)

coop(erate)

cus(tom)

depos(it)

devel(op)

dup(licate)

estab(lish)

finan(cial)

illus(tration),
illus(trate)

imag(ination),
imag(ine)

lang(uage)

leng(th)

lib(erty)

mater(ial)

of(fer)

orig(inal)

pleas(ant)

pop(ular)

pol(icy)

prej(udice)

prin(ciple),
prin(cipal)

rel(ative)

priv(ilege)

trav(el)

un(ion)

197. READING AND DICTATION PRACTICE

UNIT 26

THE ABBREVIATING PRINCIPLE
(Continued)

198. Write through the consonant following the accented syllable, if writing through the accented syllable does not give a sufficiently distinctive form.

To illustrate, writing *ab* for the word *absent* would not be sufficiently distinctive, but by writing *abs*, the word is immediately suggested. In context, *at* would not suggest *attitude* or *attribute*, but *atit* and *atrib* would furnish perfectly legible forms:

abs(ent), abs(ence)		essential (esensh)	
abso(lute)		freq(uent)	
accomp(lish)		indic(ate)	
appreciate, -tion (appresh)		journ(al)	
associa(tion) (asosh)		loc(al)	
attit(ude)		splend(id)	
benef(it)		recipr(ocate)	
canc(el)		num(erous)	
corp(oration)		ordin(ary)	
enthus(iasm)		spec(ify)	

perman(ent)		simil(ar)	
promin(ent)		social (sosh)	
pract(ice)		tit(le)	
rend(er)		tot(al)	
separ(ate)		territ(ory)	

OMISSION OF VOWEL BEFORE "SHUN"

199. The vowel is omitted in the terminations *tition, tation, dition, dation, nition, nation, mission, mation*:

repetition		consolidation	
competition		commission	
station		information	
quotation		permission	
notation		intimation	
edition		definition	
addition		combination	
condition		recognition	
foundation		destination	

200. READING AND DICTATION PRACTICE

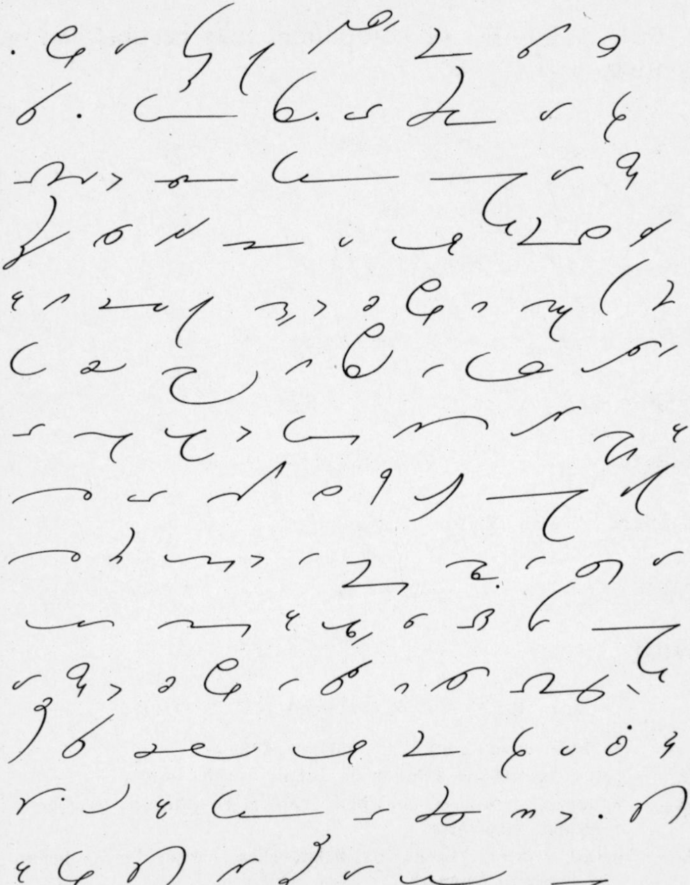

UNIT 27

COMPOUND WORDS

201. A number of compounds may be obtained by joining brief forms:

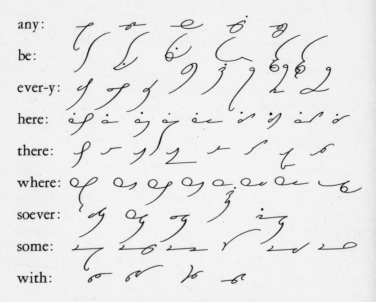

any:

be:

ever-y:

here:

there:

where:

soever:

some:

with:

202. KEY TO COMPOUND WORDS

any: anybody, anyone, anywhere, anyhow, anyway.

be: before, beforehand, behindhand, belong, beside, besides.

ever-y: whatever, whenever, whichever, however, whoever, everybody, everyone, everywhere.

here: hereafter, herein, hereinafter, hereinbefore, hereon, hereto, heretofore, hereunto, herewith.

there: thereafter, therein, therefore, therefrom, thereon, thereto, thereupon, therewith.

where: whereabouts, whereas, wherever, wherefore, wherein, whereof, whereon, elsewhere.

soever: whatsoever, wheresoever, whensoever, whosoever, whomsoever.

some: somebody, somehow, someone, sometime, somewhat, somewhere.

with: within, withstand, forthwith, notwithstanding.

NOTE: Slight modifications or omissions are made in the forms for *anywhere, anyhow, hereinafter, herewith, however, sometime, somewhere*, and the compounds beginning with *every*. These should receive special attention. The form for *notwithstanding* is *not-with-s*.

203. IRREGULAR COMPOUNDS

meanwhile   otherwise   thanksgiving

FIGURES, ETC.

204. After numerals the word *dollars* is expressed by *d*; *hundred* by *n* placed under the numeral; *thousand* by *th*; *million* by *m* placed on the line close to the numeral; *billion* by *b*; *pounds* (weight or money) by *p*; *gallons* by *g*; *barrels* by *br*; *bushels* by *bsh*; *feet* by *f*; *francs* by *fr*; *cwt.* by *nw*; *o'clock* by *o* placed over the numeral:

$5		5,000		5,000,000*	
500*		$5,000		$5,000,000	
$500		500,000		5 lbs. (or £5)	

*The sign for *hundred* is placed beneath the figure to distinguish it positively from *million*, which is written beside the figure.

500 lbs. (or £500)		5 barrels		5 o'clock	
£5,000		5 bushels		500 feet	
£500,000		5 feet		5 francs	
5 gallons		5 cwt.		500 francs	

203. The above signs may be used after the article *a* and such words as *per, few, several*:

a dollar		several hundred	
a pound		several hundred dollars	
a million		a thousand dollars	
a gallon		few thousand dollars	
per hundred		a hundred thousand	

206. *Cents* when preceded by dollars may be expressed by writing the figures representing them very small and above the numerals for the dollars; when not preceded by dollars, the sign for *s* is placed above the figures. *Per cent* is expressed by *s* written below the figures; *per cent per annum* by adding *n* to *per cent*.

$8.50	five cents	five per cent	five per cent per annum

207. READING AND DICTATION PRACTICE

[Gregg shorthand outlines]

208. WRITING PRACTICE

1. A few thousand dollars will be needed to begin the repairs on the bridge at Omaha. It is estimated that the total cost will be about $50,000.

2. Owing to the strike, the goods are coming through in very poor condition, and many of the shipments must be refused.

3. A trial of the peculiar device showed that it was not capable of developing even approximately the power claimed for it.

4. We are anxious to be invited to the private view of this new establishment, and especially of its elaborate and conspicuously beautiful decorations.

5. We are somewhat accustomed to abbreviating words in writing the English language in longhand. This expedient is especially applicable and convenient in writing rapidly. The principle is capable of great development and offers a ready means of providing easy forms for many long words that would otherwise require more elaborate and consequently less fluent outlines.

6. In the Post Office Guide it is suggested that in addressing envelopes the name of the state, written on a line by itself, is more convenient in handling the mail.

7. A peculiar situation has arisen that is likely to prejudice the development and policy of this financial institution.

8. The Reverend Mr. Smith took a conspicuously benevolent attitude toward a policy that was not likely to be successful.

9. A regular feature of the establishment was the inauguration of a fashion show each month.

CHAPTER X

UNIT 28

ANALOGICAL WORD-BEGINNINGS—DISJOINED

209. Certain prefixes or letters are disjoined to express *tr* and a following vowel. The prefix is placed above the line, very close to the remainder of the word:

centr-, center	
contr-, counter	
constr-	
detr-, deter	
distr-, destr-	
electr-, (*or* electric)	
extr-, exter, (*or* excl-)	
intr-, inter, enter, (*or* intel)	
instr-	
retr-	
restr-	

210. KEY TO ANALOGICAL WORD–BEGINNINGS

1. central, center, centralize, centralization, centrifugal.

2. contract, contrary, control, contribute, contrast, counterpart, countersign.

3. construct, construction, constrain, constraint, construe, construed.

4. detriment, detrimental, deteriorate, detract, detraction.

5. destroy, distribute, distribution, distract, distraction.

6. electric, electrical, electrolysis, electric light.

7. extra, extreme, extraordinary, exterior, extricate, exclusive, exclamation.

8. interest, interesting, enter, entered, entertain, interfere, introduce, intelligence.

9. instruct, instruction, instrument, instruments, instrumental.

10. retreat, retract, retraction, retribution, retrieve, retrogression.

11. restrain, restraint, restrict, restriction.

211. In forming the derivatives of words ending in *ct*, as in *contract*, it is not necessary to disjoin to express *ed*, *or*, *er*, or *ive*. The *t* is omitted in the primitive form (under the rules given in Chapter VIII), and also in its derivatives:

contracted		instructed	
contractor		instructor	
constructed		instructive	
constructor		extracted	
constructive		restrictive	

detracted		affected	
active		defective	
effected		detected	
effective		detective	

ANALOGICAL WORD-BEGINNINGS—COMPOUNDS

212. Some very useful forms are obtained by joining simple syllable characters, such as *in, un, dis, re, non,* to the signs for disjoined word-beginnings:

uncontrolled		redistribute	
unrestrained		disinterested	
uninteresting		indestructible	
uninstructed		inextricable	
concentration		eccentric	
reconstruction		misinterpret	

213. READING AND DICTATION PRACTICE

UNIT 29

214. ANALOGICAL WORD-BEGINNINGS—DISJOINED
(Continued)

agr-
  aggr-

ant-

decl-

incl-

magn-
  (*or* Mc)

multi

over

para*

post*

recl-

self, circu,
  circum

grand

*The prefix *para* is written above the rest of the word; *post* is written on
the line close before the following character.

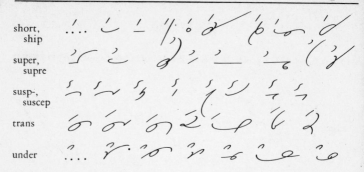

short, ship	
super, supre	
susp-, suscep	
trans	
under	

215. KEY TO ANALOGICAL WORD-BEGINNINGS

1. agree, agreeable, agreement, agriculture, aggravate, aggressive, disagree, disagreeable.

2. anticipate, anticipation, antagonize, antecedent, anterior.

3. declare, declaration, decline, declined, declaim, declamation.

4. include, incline, inclination, inclined, inclusion, inclusive, inclement.

5. magnify, magnitude, magnificent, magnet, McNeil.

6. multitude, multiple, multiply, multiplication.

7. over, overlook, overtake, overcoat, overthrow, overcome.

8. paragraph, parallel, paramount, paradise, paralysis, parasite.

9. postage, postal, postmaster, postpone, postman.

10. recline, reclined, reclaim, reclamation, recluse.

11. selfish, self-confident, self-control, circular, circulation, circumstances, circus.

12. grand, grandson, granddaughter, grandmother, grandfather.

13. short, shorter, shorten, shortage, shortly, shortsighted, shipshape, shipwreck, shipyard.

14. superintend, superior, supervise, support, supreme, supremacy, superb, supersede.

15. suspect, suspected, suspicious, suspicion, susceptible, suspend, suspense, suspension.

16. transact, transacted, transaction, transfer, translation, transport, transfix.

17. under, understanding, undertake, understood, underneath, underline, underwrite.

216. ANALOGICAL WORD-BEGINNINGS—COMPOUNDS

(Continued)

self-interest		disinclined	
unselfish		disinclination	
unparalleled		self-contradiction	
unsuspected		unsusceptible	
self-control		untransacted	
unsuspicious		unrestricted	

217. READING AND DICTATION PRACTICE

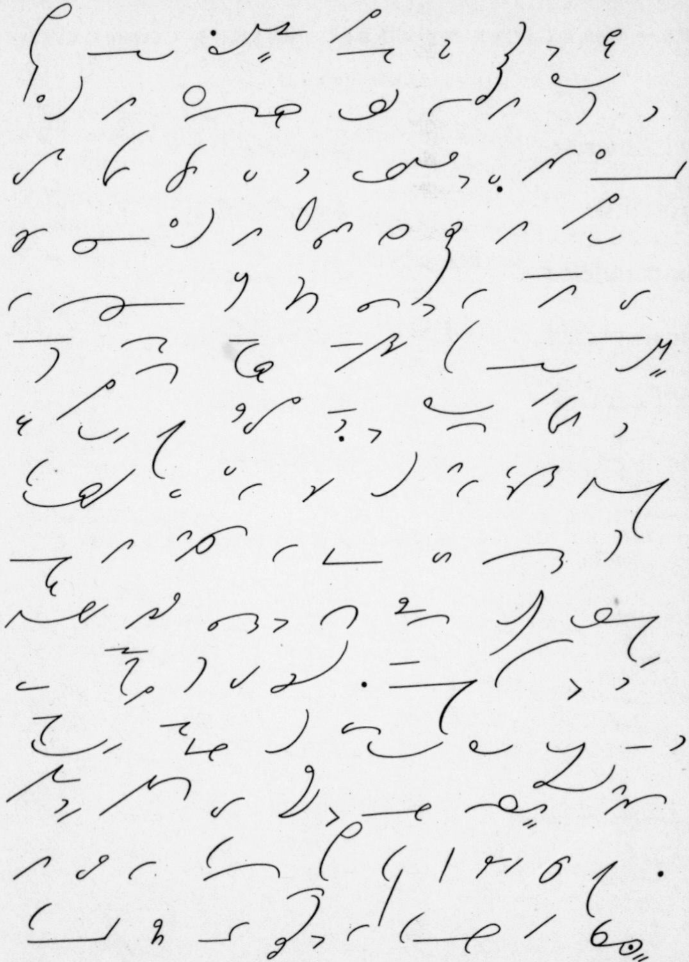

UNIT 30

PHRASING PRINCIPLES

218. The words *misunderstand* and *misunderstood* are expressed by *stand* and *stood* placed under *mis*, with *mis* placed on the line of writing. This rule is extended to the words *understand* and *understood* when they are preceded by a pronoun, a brief form, or a short phrase form:

misunderstand

I understand

misunderstood

I do not understand

I understood

I cannot understand

we understood

thoroughly understood

219. The words *extra, enter, over, under, short, center, counter, agree, grand* are expressed by the prefixal forms placed over the next word:

extra discount

under consideration

enter the

extra fare

enter into

short time

over the

center line

under any

agree with you

220. The word *done* is expressed by the *den* blend in many phrases:

have done		will be done	
has been done		would be done	
has done		should be done	

221. In many phrases the word *than* is expressed by *n*:

quicker than		rather than	
better than		nearer than	
sooner than		greater than	

222. Many useful business phrases may be secured by slightly modifying the form for *us*:

give us		to us	
tell us		let us	
write us		mail us	

223. In many phrases *department* is expressed by a disjoined *d*:

credit department		purchasing department	
shipping department		accounting department	

224. In a number of phrases the word forms are modified or a word is omitted where the grammatical construction of the sentence would compel its restoration when transcribing:

of course		whether or not	
at once		at all events	
at any rate		to some extent	
great deal		to a great extent	
I always		to such an extent	
on hand		at the same time	
as follows		in other words	
whole lot		once in a while	
one another		in my opinion	
day's sight		in the first place	
do you know		as soon as possible	
great pleasure		as a matter of fact	
your order		on account of the fact	
first class		over and over again	

225. READING AND DICTATION PRACTICE

226. WRITING PRACTICE

1. The supreme test of his intelligent understanding of the transaction was revealed in his superior statement regarding it.

2. A shortage in the shipment was discovered by the superintendent, who immediately took the matter up with his superior.

3. We suspect that the error in judgment was due entirely to his susceptible and unsuspicious nature, as well as to his shortsightedness.

4. We shall not overlook his tendency to overcharge our batteries, something that will be overcome by the simple expedient of giving the undertaking to McLain.

5. The instructor attempted to restrain his students from further controversy about the peculiar effects of electrolysis, to say nothing of the heated discussion about centrifugal and centripetal forces.

6. His disinterested attitude led to an unparalleled controversy.

7. Mr. McFadden seemed disinclined to enter into the agreement owing to the aggressive policy and the superior air of the gentleman representing the Paramount Overcoat Corporation.

8. The transfer of the contract may be easily effected, but I am inclined to think that it will be disadvantageous.

9. Both the interior and exterior finishes were designed by Mr. McLaren, of McLaren, McNamara & McIntyre.

10. The reconstruction of the dam was resisted by a multitude of citizens because of the extraordinary declivity of the adjacent walls of the cliff, which would necessitate much extra construction.

CHAPTER XI

UNIT 31

227. ANALOGICAL WORD-ENDINGS—JOINED

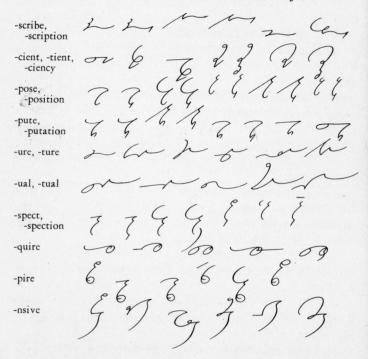

-scribe, -scription

-cient, -tient, -ciency

-pose, -position

-pute, -putation

-ure, -ture

-ual, -tual

-spect, -spection

-quire

-pire

-nsive

NOTE: Occasionally a disjoined prefix precedes a joined suffix, as in *circumspect*, *introspect*, in which case the disjoined sign is written above.

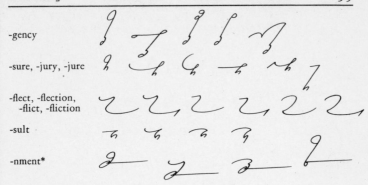

-gency

-sure, -jury, -jure

-flect, -flection, -flict, -fliction

-sult

-nment*

*The "jog" is omitted in the termination *-nment*.

228. KEY TO ANALOGICAL WORD-ENDINGS

1. subscribe, subscription, describe, description, inscribe, prescription.

2. ancient, patient, impatient, efficient, efficiency, deficient, deficiency.

3. compose, composition, propose, proposition, suppose, supposition, dispose, disposition, oppose, opposition.

4. repute, reputation, dispute, disputation, compute, computation, impute, amputation.

5. secure, picture, feature, nature, creature, departure.

6. actual, mutual, equal, eventual, continual.

7. inspect, inspection, prospect, prospective, expectation, circumspect, introspection.

8. require, inquire, acquire, requirement, acquires.

9. expire, inspire, conspire, transpire, perspire, aspire.

10. expensive, extensive, comprehensive, offensive, intensive, defensive.

11. agency, emergency, exigency, urgency, contingency.

12. assure, leisure, pressure, measure, treasure, injure.

13. reflect, reflection, inflict, infliction, conflict, confliction.

14. insult, result, consult, consultation.

15. assignment, refinement, consignment, adjournment.

229. READING AND DICTATION PRACTICE

UNIT 32

ANALOGICAL WORD-ENDINGS—DISJOINED

230. In most of the disjoined word-endings the vowel preceding the ending is understood, as in *art(i)cle, barn(a)cle, dom(e)stic, cal(a)mity, extr(e)mity, auth(o)rity, sec(u)rity*:

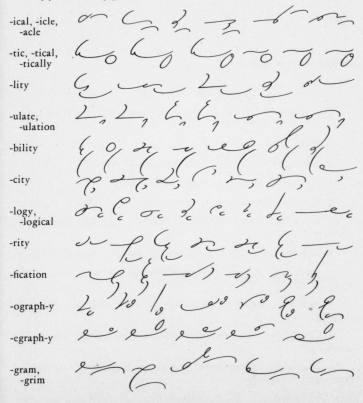

-ical, -icle, -acle

-tic, -tical, -tically

-lity

-ulate, -ulation

-bility

-city

-logy, -logical

-rity

-fication

-ograph-y

-egraph-y

-gram, -grim

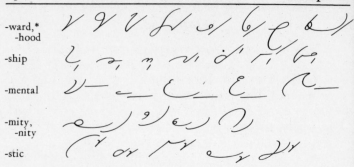

-ward,*
 -hood

-ship

-mental

-mity,
 -nity

-stic

*In the words *forward*, *afterward*, *upward*, *backward* the suffix is joined; in other words, it is disjoined.

231. KEY TO ANALOGICAL WORD-ENDINGS

1. article, practical, physical, musical, medical, technical.

2. politic, political, politically, critic, critical, critically.

3. personality, locality, formality, facility, utility.

4. formulate, formulation, speculate, speculation, regulate, regulation.

5. possibility, ability, sensibility, nobility, reliability, adaptability, visibility.

6. capacity, simplicity, ferocity, tenacity, scarcity, sagacity, electricity.

7. psychology, apology, analogy, physiology, theology, zoölogy, genealogy, mineralogy.

8. authority, majority, prosperity, security, sincerity, popularity, minority.

9. classification, specification, modification, notification, qualification, justification.

10. phonograph, photography, geography lithography, stenography, typography, typographic.

11. telegraph, telegraphy, telegrapher, telegraphic, calligraphy.

12. telegram, cablegram, radiogram, pilgrim, program.

13. forward, afterward, upward, backward, reward, boyhood, neighbor-hood, childhood.

14. friendship, kinship, worship, courtship, hardship, township, part-nership.

15. fundamental, ornamental, supplemental, experimental, temperamental.

16. calamity, extremity, serenity, divinity.

17. domestic, artistic, drastic, elastic, fantastic.

232. READING AND DICTATION PRACTICE

(shorthand outlines)

UNIT 33

INITIALS

233. As there is no context to initials, accuracy in writing them is of prime importance:

A		H		O		V	
B		I		P		W	
C		J		Q		X	
D		K		R		Y	
E		L		S		Z	
F		M		T			
G		N		U			

234. Many writers prefer to write initials in longhand, and if this is done, a great saving in time may be effected by writing them in small letters and joining the letters, thus:

A. B. Smith   C. D. Brown   E. F. Jones

INTERSECTION

235. The expedient known as intersection, or the writing of one character through another, is sometimes useful for special phrases. In applying this expedient the writer must rely very largely upon his own judgment. In his daily work as stenographer or reporter he may find some terms peculiar to the business in which he is engaged occurring so frequently that special forms may be adopted for them that will be brief and yet absolutely distinctive. Very often the writing of one character through another will meet the exigency. The following are useful examples:

A. D.		Associated Press	
A. M.		Democratic party	
P. M.		Republican party	
C. O. D.		political party	
price list		Baltimore & Ohio (B. & O.)	
list price		New York Central	
vice versa		Michigan Central	
bank draft		Illinois Central	
order blank		endowment policy	

Grand Trunk		indemnity policy	
selling price		Canadian Pacific	
market price		Northern Pacific	
Union Pacific		application blank	
School Board		bond and mortgage	
member banks		chairman of the board	
curb market		Federal Reserve Board	
stock market		Board of Managers	
Great Britain		Board of Management	
enclosed blank		commercial paper	
General Manager		account current	
Assistant General Manager		chattel mortgage	
bills payable		certificate of deposit	
bills receivable		commercial draft	
profit and loss		Board of Education	
Board of Trade		Chamber of Commerce	

236. READING AND DICTATION PRACTICE

237. WRITING PRACTICE

1. It transpired that he did not aspire to the office himself but was conspiring to overthrow the incumbent.

2. Intensive study of the actual conditions of the conflict ought to make it possible to prevent the recurrence of this emergency.

3. Without a considerable body of experimental data it is impossible to formulate physiological rules with reliability.

4. In the extremity, the sublimity and nobility of his character were revealed with inspiring clarity.

5. The floods were a national calamity in which thousands were injured, to say nothing of the financial losses inflicted on all the people in that territory.

6. It will probably require the services of many stenographers to answer all the inquiries about the branches of this extensive business, and I myself shall take care of those of great urgency.

7. One of the finest things a teacher can do is to inspire the student to make proper use of his leisure time, to give some time to reflection and thought.

8. Nobility of thought, adaptability of ideas, and generosity of nature—these are the fundamental requisites for those who would have the real rewards of life.

9. His phraseology seems to call for an apology on his part; the other members of the partnership were not backward in sending him a notification to that effect.

10. He employed all his great ability in writing an interesting article on the politics of this locality. As he wrote with authority, and had every justification for what he said, his article had a certain degree of popularity with the majority.

CHAPTER XII

UNIT 34

STATES AND TERRITORIES

238. The abbreviations used in the following list are those adopted by the Post Office Department:

Ala.		Hawaii		Minn.	
Alaska		Idaho		Miss.	
Ariz.		Ill.		Mo.	
Ark.		Ind.		Mont.	
Calif.		Iowa		Nebr.	
Colo.		Kans.		Nev.	
Conn.		Ky.		N. H.	
Del.		La.		N. J.	
D. C.		Maine		N. Mex.	
Fla.		Md.		N. Y.	
Ga.		Mass.		N. C.	
Guam		Mich.		N. Dak.	

Ohio	⌣	R. I.	⌒	Vt.	⟩
Okla.	⌒⌒	S. C.	⌒⌒	Va.	⟩
Oreg.	⌣	S. Dak.	⟋⌒	Wash.	⟩
Pa.	6	Tenn.	⌒	W. Va.	⟩
P. I.	⟨⌒	Tex.	⌒	Wis.	⟩
P. R.	⟨	Utah	⟋⌒	Wyo.	⟩ .

PRINCIPAL CITIES OF THE UNITED STATES

239. The following names of cities are arranged in the order of their population:

New York	⌒	Boston	⟨
Chicago	⟋	Pittsburgh	⟨⟩
Philadelphia	⌒⌒	San Francisco	⟩
Los Angeles	⌣⟩	Buffalo	⟩
Detroit	⟋	Washington	⟩
Cleveland	⌒⟩	Milwaukee	⌒
St. Louis	⌒⌒	Newark	⌒
Baltimore	⟨	Minneapolis	⌒⟩

New Orleans	Atlanta
Cincinnati	Akron
Kansas City	Birmingham
Seattle	Omaha
Indianapolis	Dallas
St. Paul	San Antonio
Portland	Syracuse
Louisville	Worcester
Jersey City	Richmond
Rochester	Memphis
Toledo	New Haven
Columbus	Dayton
Denver	Norfolk
Providence	Youngstown
Houston	Hartford
Oakland	Ft. Worth

Tulsa		Camden	
Grand Rapids		Fall River	
Oklahoma City		Wilmington	
Bridgeport		Cambridge	
Miami		Yonkers	
Long Beach		Albany	
Des Moines		San Diego	
Springfield		New Bedford	
Flint		Lowell	
Paterson		Reading	
Scranton		Duluth	
Erie		Elizabeth	
Jacksonville		Canton	
Nashville		El Paso	
Trenton		Spokane	
Salt Lake City		Tacoma	

240. READING AND DICTATION PRACTICE

UNIT 35

NAME TERMINATIONS

241. The terminations *burg, ville, field, port* may generally be expressed by the first letter, joined or disjoined as convenient; *ford*, by *fd*; *ington*, by a disjoined *tn*; and *ingham*, by a disjoined *m*:

Harrisburg		Davenport	
Petersburg		Newport	
Fitchburg		Shreveport	
Newburgh		Oxford	
Danville		Rockford	
Zanesville		Milford	
Evansville		Kensington	
Knoxville		Arlington	
Pittsfield		Birmingham	
Plainfield		Nottingham	

NOTE: A distinction between *ton* and *town* is made as follows:

Johnston	Johnstown	Charleston	Charlestown

242. The names of cities and states often may be joined:

Buffalo, N. Y.		St. Louis, Mo.	
St. Paul, Minn.		Rochester, N. Y.	
Boston, Mass.		Baltimore, Md.	
Detroit, Mich.		Memphis, Tenn.	
Chicago, Ill.		Louisville, Ky.	
Denver, Colo.		Minneapolis, Minn.	
Omaha, Nebr.		Washington, D. C.	

"STATE OF" JOINED

243. When the words "State of" precede the name of a state, omit *of* and join the words, if convenient:

State of N. Y.		State of Mass.	
State of Nebr.		State of Pa.	
State of Ill.		State of La.	
State of N. J.		State of Ga.	
State of Miss.		State of Minn.	

244. CANADIAN PROVINCES AND CITIES
(Including Newfoundland and Labrador)

Prince Edward Island		Edmonton	
Nova Scotia		Hamilton	
New Brunswick		London	
Quebec		Montreal	
Ontario		Ottawa	
Manitoba		Peterboro	
Saskatchewan		Regina	
Alberta		St. John	
British Columbia		Saskatoon	
Yukon		Toronto	
N. W. Territories		Vancouver	
Labrador		Victoria	
Newfoundland		Windsor	
Brantford		Winnipeg	
Calgary		Saint John's	

245. READING AND DICTATION PRACTICE

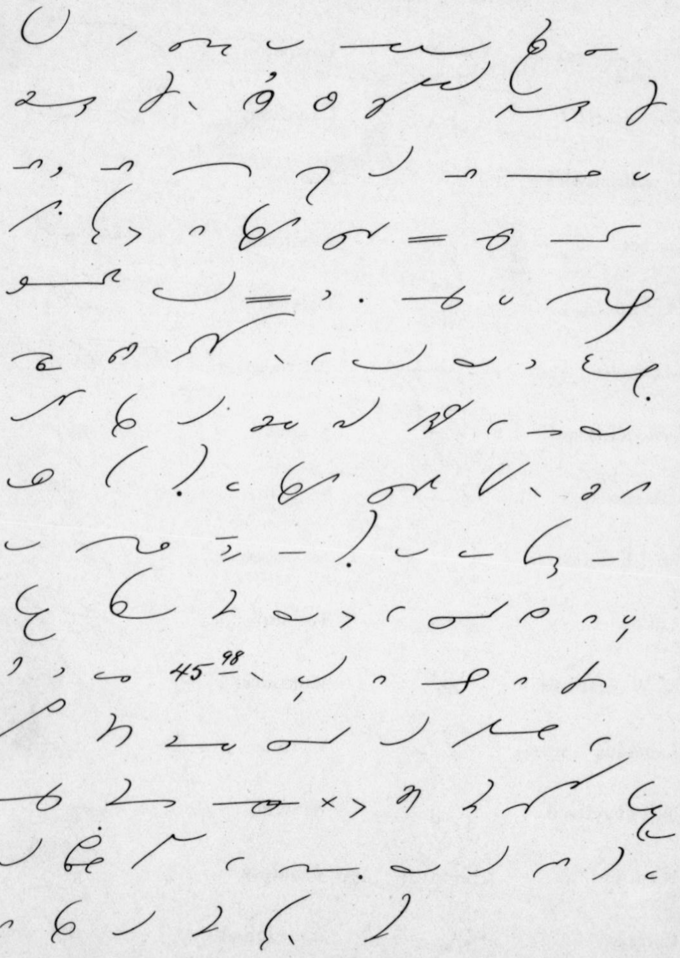

UNIT 36

A SHORT VOCABULARY

246. This short vocabulary will be a valuable addition to the equipment of every shorthand writer. Though many of these words are not of high frequency, it will be seen at a glance that they are of sufficient importance to warrant study. Many of them are written according to the abbreviating principle:

A	abstract		assist	
	accommodation		Atlantic	
	accompany		attach	
	administration		attorney	
	affidavit		attract	
	afraid		authoritative	
	American		automobile	
	application		avoid	
	approval	**B**	bankrupt	
	architect		bookkeeper	
	argument		bureau	

C					
	Christmas		corporation	
	citizen		coupon	
	civil		crop	
	clerk		cultivate	
	commerce		curious	
	commercial	**D**	deceive	
	compare		default	
	comparative		defendant	
	consequent, consequence		democrat	
	conclude		designate	
	conclusion		disagreement	
	congress		disappoint	
	connect		discuss	
	conspicuous		distinct	
	constitution		distinguish	
	conversation		disturb	

	doctrine		**H**	headquarters	
E	emphasize			husband	
	energy		**I**	inasmuch	
	English			inaugurate	
	entitle			independent, independence	
	estate			indispensable	
	exchange			institute	
	execute			investigate	
	exercise		**J**	junior	
F	familiar			jury	
	fault		**L**	legislate	
	fortune			legislation	
	freight			legislative	
	fulfill			legislator	
G	glorious			legislature	
	God			likewise	

	literary			obstruct	
	literature			obvious	
	litigation			occupy, occupation	
	locate		**P**	Pacific	
	luxury			parcel	
M	manufacture			partial	
	merchant			passenger	
	messenger			patron	
	misdemeanor			pattern	
	mortgage			persecute	
N	neglect			plaintiff	
	negligence			practical	
	negligent			practice	
	negotiate			premium	
	novelty			probability	
O	observe			property	

	prosecute	
	publication	
	punctual	
	pupil	
	push	
Q	qualify	
R	remainder	
	resignation	
S	salesman	
	scarce	
	secretary	
	signature	
	significant, significance	
	silence	
	specify	
	specific	

	society	
	subsequent	
	substitute	
	succeed	
	sympathy	
T	testimonial	
	testimony	
	text	
U	unavoidable	
	universal	
V	variety	
	verdict	
	vote	
W	warehouse	
	wholesale	
	wife	

247. READING AND DICTATION PRACTICE

[Shorthand outlines]

7270   )   18

1008

2008

1008,

248. WRITING PRACTICE

1. Of the 61 aircraft-production establishments reporting to the U. S. Department of Commerce in 1927, 15 were located in New York; 9 each in California and Michigan; 4 each in Illinois, Missouri, and Ohio; 3 each in New Jersey and Pennsylvania; 2 in Maryland and 1 each in Colorado, Connecticut, Iowa, Kansas, Nebraska, Virginia, Washington, and Wisconsin.

2. There were 4,134 civilian-owned aircraft, including balloons, airplanes, and airships. California led with more than 600; New York second with 387; Illinois, 350; Michigan, 291; Texas, 261; Ohio, 231; Missouri, 216; and Pennsylvania, 212.

3. Air mail is rapidly securing the business that always goes to the fastest method of transportation. Illustrative of the difference in transportation time between train and air-mail planes is the following schedule: New York to San Francisco, train 83 hours, air mail 31 hours; Chicago to New York, train 20 hours, air mail 9 hours; St. Paul to Dallas, train 37 hours, air mail 17 hours; Boston to Cleveland, train 16 hours, air mail 8 hours; Los Angeles to St. Louis, train 60 hours, air mail 26 hours.

4. The average rise and fall of tide at the important American seaports is as follows: Baltimore, 1 foot, 2 inches; Boston, 9 feet, 7 inches; Galveston, 1 foot;

New Orleans, none; New York, 4 feet, 5 inches; Philadelphia, 5 feet, 2 inches; San Francisco, 3 feet, 11 inches; and Washington, D. C., 2 feet, 11 inches.

5. The English lady was obliged to abandon her plan to celebrate Christmas on this side of the Atlantic with her son, who was a Junior at college.

6. It is obvious that failure to observe the terms of the mortgage constitutes a default in the agreement.

7. The well-nigh universal and wholesale use of the automobile has added greatly to the comfort and luxury of living.

8. The merchant notified his salesmen that all the goods stored in the warehouse were to be put on sale.

9. Three classes of employees were affected by the notice—secretaries, bookkeepers, and general clerks.

10. In consequence of the disagreement between the plaintiff and his attorney, the jury heard no testimony that day.

11. It was a distinct disappointment to the distinguished literary light not to be included on the program.

12. The messenger made a frantic effort to locate the parcel containing the testimonials regarding the texts.

INDEX*

*Index of Brief Forms follows the general index.

For prefixes, suffixes, and words used in phrases see under "Prefixes," "Suffixes," and "Phrasing."

INDEX TO BRIEF FORMS

171

SOME GREGG PUBLICATIONS

SHORTHAND (BASIC BOOKS)

Gregg Shorthand Manual. Gregg 1.50

Gregg Speed Studies. Gregg. A combined textbook and dictation course. A companion to the Manual............................ 1.20

Graded Readings in Gregg Shorthand. Hunter. A reading book adapted to early dictation.. .75

Gregg Speed Studies—Graded Readings in Gregg Shorthand, Combined Edition. Gregg and Hunter.................................... 1.50

Gregg Speed Building. Gregg. An advanced text for use upon the completion of the Manual.. 1.20

An Introduction to Transcription. Adams and Skimin............... .60

Rational Dictation. McNamara and Markett........................ 1.40

Direct-Method Materials for Gregg Shorthand. Brewington and Soutter 1.72

Gregg Shorthand Manual for the Functional Method. Leslie. In two volumes, each 1.50

Direct-Practice Units for Beginning Gregg Shorthand. Odell, Rowe, and Stuart .... .60

Fundamental Drills in Gregg Shorthand. Beers and Scott. Sentences, paragraphs, letters, and articles in shorthand, graded according to the units of the Gregg Shorthand Manual............................ 1.20

SHORTHAND (SUPPLEMENTARY)

Gregg Shorthand Dictionary. Containing the outlines of nearly 17,000 words 1.50

Gregg Shorthand Phrase Book. Contains about 3,000 useful phrases. A great aid in attaining speed 1.00

Progressive Exercises in Gregg Shorthand. Tests students' knowledge of each lesson.. .50

Word and Sentence Drills in Gregg Shorthand. Markett. Contains list of words, sentences, and letters illustrating the principles as set forth in the Manual. All in type .... .60

Dictation for Beginners. Bisbee. Contains sentences and letters based on the principles of the Manual. Graded by units instead of by chapters. All in type .... .72

Five Thousand Most-Used Shorthand Forms. Gregg. Arranged according to paragraphs in the Manual.................................. .60

Progressive Dictation. Wilson. Sentences and letters graded according to the thirty-six units of the Manual............................. .56

Short Business Letters for Dictation. Gross. Contains 580 short letters, none of which is over sixty words in length. All in type.......... .60

Intensive Exercises in Shorthand Vocabulary Building. Swem. Twenty scientifically constructed dictation exercises employing the 1,000 most-used words .... .76

SHORTHAND (FOREIGN LANGUAGE ADAPTATIONS)

Afrikaans	1.00	**Italian**	1.00
Esperanto	.40	**Polish**	1.00
French (Senecal)	1.50	**Portuguese**	1.00
German	1.00	**Russian**	1.00
Irish	1.00	**Spanish**	1.50

SHORTHAND (FOR THE REPORTER)

Gregg Reporting Shortcuts. Gregg. A collection of reporting phrases and shortcuts compiled from the work of expert writers............ 2.00

The Stenographic Expert. (Gregg Edition.) Bottome. Adapted to Gregg Shorthand by John Robert Gregg 2.00

Gregg Medical Shorthand Manual for Stenographers, Secretaries, and Reporters. Smither 2.00

Gregg Shorthand Reporting Course. Swem and Gregg. 20 pamphlets, each 40c; complete set, $6.40; bound text........................ 7.00

SHORTHAND (FOR THE TEACHER)

Teaching Principles and Procedures for Gregg Shorthand. Skene, Walsh, and Lomax. A methods and source book for the teacher of Gregg Shorthand 1.20

Daily Lesson Plans for Teaching Gregg Shorthand by the Sentence Method. Zinman, Strelsin, and Weitz............................. 1.20

Teaching Gregg Shorthand by the Analytical Method. Frick. A teacher's methods and source book for elementary shorthand 1.20

Diagnostic Testing and Remedial Teaching of Gregg Shorthand. Rollinson. A presentation of the modern method of testing............. 2.00

The Teaching of Shorthand: Some Suggestions to Young Teachers. Gregg. Contains valuable hints on pedagogy and classroom methods.. .80

The Teaching of Gregg Shorthand by the Functional Method. Leslie.... 1.20

Teacher's Handbook for the Functional Method. Leslie .... .40

Teacher's Manual for Direct-Practice Units for Beginning Gregg Shorthand. Odell, Rowe, and Stuart................................net .25

The Basic Principles of Gregg Shorthand. Gregg. A complete, scientific discussion of the fundamental principles of Gregg Shorthand........ 1.00

SHORTHAND (READING BOOKS)

Alice in Wonderland	.60	The Great Stone Face	.28
Letters of a Self-Made Merchant to His Son	.28	The Legend of Sleepy Hollow..	.28
		Rip Van Winkle	.28
The Diamond Necklace	.28	Hamlet. As told by Lamb	.28
The Man Without a Country....	.28	Creeds of Great Business Men..	.28
A Christmas Carol	.28		

SECRETARIAL PRACTICE

Applied Secretarial Practice. SoRelle and Gregg. Text 1.40

    Laboratory Materials .... .60

ENGLISH AND SPELLING

The English of Business, Complete. Hagar, Wilson, Hutchinson, and Blanchard. Text, $1. Work Book .... .40

Correlated Studies in Stenography. Lawrence, McAfee, and Butler. A correlated course in shorthand, business English, and correspondence 1.20

Business Letters: Functions, Principles, Composition. Johns. The case method of presentation 1.40

20,000 Words—Spelled, Divided, and Accented. Leslie .... .60

Words: Their Spelling, Punctuation, Definition, and Application. Second Revised Edition. SoRelle and Kitt............................. .44

TYPEWRITING

Gregg Typing, Techniques and Projects. SoRelle and Smith. A new series of typing texts featuring the Rational method, introducing new pedagogic procedures.

Gregg Typing, Book I. Completes the entire cycle of typing theory in 180 periods 1.20

Gregg Typing, Book II. The advanced course, containing a second cycle of applied typing skill on a higher level of accomplishment 1.20

Gregg Typing, Complete Course. Books I and II bound under one cover . . 1.50

Gregg Typing, College Course. Prepared especially for use in private schools and institutions of higher learning 1.20

Gregg Typing, Intensive Course. An intensive course for evening-school, part-time, and other short vocational courses 1.00

Typewriting Technique. Smith. A short, easy course for the development of superior typing skill 1.00

Rational Typewriting Projects. SoRelle. For advanced typing classes . . 1.20

Typewriting Speed Studies. Hakes 52

The Technique of Teaching Typewriting. Clem. A textbook for students training to become teachers of typewriting 2.00

Learning to Typewrite. Book. Presents the results of an analysis of the processes involved in the learning of typewriting 2.40

The Psychology of Skill. Book 2.00

COMMERCIAL SUBJECTS

Business Organization and Administration. de Haas 1.40

Essentials of Commercial Law, Revised Edition. Whigam, Jones, and Moody 1.40

Business Mathematics—Exercises, Problems, and Tests. Rosenberg. In pad form, 8½ x 11 inches in size. In two parts. Part I, 60c; Part II, .80

Business Mathematics—Principles and Practice. Rosenberg 1.40

Essentials of Business Mathematics—Principles and Practice. Rosenberg 1.20

Intensive Bookkeeping and Accounting. Fearon 1.80

Bookkeeping and Accounting Practice. Lenert and McNamara 1.50

Our Business Life. Jones. A first course in business for eighth- or ninth-grade pupils. Provides information, exploration, guidance, business practice—a foundation for the future study of business subjects 1.50

SALESMANSHIP AND ADVERTISING

Salesmanship for Everybody. Ely and Starch 1.40

Understanding Advertising. Hawley and Zabin 1.20

Personality: Studies in Personal Development. Spillman 1.34

MISCELLANEOUS

Gregg Spiral Notebook. A perfect notebook. Opens flat at every page. Covers serve as "copyholder" in transcribing. "Easy-read ruling."

The Business Education World. A monthly magazine for teachers. Yearly subscription price . . . . net 1.00

The Gregg Writer. A monthly magazine. Yearly subscription price . . net 1.50

THE GREGG PUBLISHING COMPANY

New York   Chicago   Boston   San Francisco
    Toronto   London   Sydney